EMBRACING LIFE, SPIRIT, FAITH, AND ADVERSITY

THE GIFTS OF FREEDOM SERIES

Embracing Life, Spirit, Faith, and Adversity

Book 1

The Gifts of Freedom Series

Greg Rice

DESTINY IMAGE® PUBLISHERS, INC.
P.O. Box 310, Shippensburg, PA 17257-0310

"Speaking to the Purposes of God for this Generation and for the Generations to Come."

This book and all other Destiny Image, Revival Press, Mercy Place, Fresh Bread, Destiny Image Fiction, and Treasure House books are available at Christian bookstores and distributors worldwide.

For a U.S. bookstore nearest you, call **1-800-722-6774.**

For more information on foreign distributors, call **717-532-3040.**

Reach us on the Internet: **www.destinyimage.com.**

ISBN 10: 0-7684-2707-X

ISBN 13: 978-0-7684-2707-3

For Worldwide Distribution, Printed in the U.S.A.

1 2 3 4 5 6 7 8 9 10 11 / 12 11 10 09 08

DEDICATED TO

MY SON, ROBERT RICE

and men and women who are spiritual paupers,
men and women behind bars, men and women in rehab,

and

You.

I pray that through this book you will gain greater freedom,
a deeper understanding of God, and a closer relationship with Him.

CONTENTS

PREFACE

I started writing *The Gifts of Freedom* for my son and other men and women in prisons around the world. While these men and women are lacking physical freedom within cement walls, confined to caged cells, this book was written to help set them free in the most important place— the heart. Walking with Jesus Christ and finding intimacy with God and His Spirit is true freedom that cement and steel cannot restrain. Indeed, many who have found this spiritual freedom have also found a miraculous physical freedom.

Yet, as God was guiding me and shaping my writing, I realized that it isn't just the prison system that keeps people jailed in some kind of involuntary restraint. The largest "jails" in the world are full of many law-abiding citizens. I'm talking about people who are serving a sentence of loneliness, guilt, sorrow, hopelessness, fear, despair, poverty, sickness, disease, anger, confusion, addiction, depression, or lack of purpose and meaning just to name a few. *And sadly, even churches are full of people who have not acted on receiving the Gifts of Freedom God offers.*

Consider your own life. Are you living out your own life sentence? Are you restrained in some areas from living life in the full freedoms God desires for you? Maybe steel bars aren't keeping you from living fully free;

but isn't the impact just as devastating? Couldn't prison be defined as "a life void of its intended freedoms, a life restrained, a life withheld from the abundance God desires for us"? If you are serving this kind of sentence, ask yourself: is this really life?

No. Absolutely not!

But here's the good news. Jesus Christ died to offer you His wonderful Gifts of Freedom designed to set you spiritually free. Will you choose to receive, unwrap, and use all of them to their fullest? In this series of books we'll explore the life-changing power of God's gifts—gifts for living an abundant, spiritually free life that may even produce physical freedoms.

If you are looking to read something that's full of gimmicks, short cuts, and tricks to help you make little changes for a better life—then you're holding the wrong book. Jesus shed His blood for you and me to radically change and transform our lives. In fact, He offered to take our sentences from us. Jesus doesn't offer a temporary fix, but rather a new life. What I've illuminated in these books are God's Gifts of Freedom for those who want to revolutionize their lives. Is that you?

The chapters in this series of three books present 12 gifts that build up to the best Gift of all—God Himself. However, this information is only the beginning. The true impact of these books will happen where they end and *you begin.*

Will you choose to receive, unwrap, and use His gifts?

INTRODUCTION

✠ *So He [Jesus] came to a town in Samaria called Sychar, near the plot of ground Jacob had given to his son Joseph. Jacob's well was there, and Jesus, tired as He was from the journey, sat down by the well. It was about the sixth hour. When a Samaritan woman came to draw water, Jesus said to her, "Will you give me a drink?" (His disciples had gone into the town to buy food.) The Samaritan woman said to Him, "You are a Jew and I am a Samaritan woman. How can you ask me for a drink?" (For Jews do not associate with Samaritans.) Jesus answered her, "If you knew the gift of God and who it is that asks you for a drink, you would have asked Him and He would have given you living water"* (John 4:5-10).

The Bible has been printed more than any book in history; however, most people don't really understand it. It is my goal to help you explore some of what the Bible teaches and to offer you a better understanding of its message. For instance, what is "the *gift*" this verse is referring to? And what do we need to know about who Jesus is to receive this living water? Or, what kind of freedoms do we obtain when we have received this living water?

What you learn will change your life. The key to this change is being willing to take the time to examine the Bible and listen to what God has to say to you through its pages—His Word. Consider how much time you spend on things that are only temporary. The message of the Bible—and its potential impact on your life—is *eternal*. It's worth the time to know its message for you.

If you were given the gift of a computer and an e-mail account, but didn't take the time to learn how to use them, then you couldn't use these potentially life-changing tools. Many people who are *set in their ways* don't take the time to learn, and some just don't want to exert the effort. To benefit from gifts, you must take time to learn about them.

Take a moment to read again the Bible passage at the beginning of this chapter. Samaritans were half-breeds, outcasts whom Jesus' contemporaries would have gone out of their way to avoid. But Jesus didn't avoid this woman—instead, He engaged her in a conversation that would change her entire perspective on life. Jesus offers you the same gift He offered the woman at the well: the Gifts of Freedom.

God offers us invisible gifts that are receivable and quite usable if we take the time to understand them. Some are physical gifts and some are spiritual—all give you new freedoms. Consider the natural law of gravity, which is a great gift that you can count on every day to keep the earth in its orbit and your feet on the ground. Over time and with study, scientists have unwrapped the ability to harness gravity's power by building dams and hydroelectric plants that use gravity to create electricity to light cities. Because of their deeper understanding of gravity, we have more freedom to use the night as well as power speeding trains which, in turn, provide more freedom of time and places to go. You have to be consciously aware of how this invisible law of gravity operates and how it has a profound effect on your everyday life. Though you *can't see it*, you *can* see and rely on its effects. You organize and adjust your life counting on and considering its effects. This is why you don't step off of a high ledge—you know how gravity would respond to that choice!

There are likewise unseen *spiritual* laws which are just as certain and even more significant and powerful than gravity. These spiritual laws that affect you daily are spoken of in the Bible. There is power in these laws which can bring great freedom to you, but in order to receive that benefit from them—to receive the Gifts of Freedom—we have to understand these laws and our Creator's ultimate purpose for each of us.

Humankind was created to interact in love and friendship with the Creator. You specifically, were created out of God's desire to have companionship with His creation, an intimacy in our very interactions with one another that was designed to produce pure love—the God kind of love that has no restrictions or end.

The problem—people don't take the time to get to know God. Do you think you could have true companionship with someone who doesn't know you? Who doesn't spend the effort to get to know you? Or who just assumes they know you based on rumors or what other people may say? In a marriage, could you find real love with your spouse if they try to force you to be someone you're not? Of course not. That would make for relational disaster. But, this is how some people think about God. They don't really know Him. Not being familiar with what the Bible says about God, about who He is and what His nature is, they make Him into the kind of God they *want* Him to be. Therefore, they wind up not becoming a true *companion* of His.

How much do you know about the God of the Bible? Do you think God would say you have been His good companion? Do you really think you *know* how to be a good companion to God? I am going to answer these questions and many more by exploring the Bible and helping you discover what the Bible says about just who God is, what His nature is, and what He desires. More importantly, I am even going to show you how to get specific answers about your life *directly* from God—answers *only He* can give you.

At the end of each chapter, you'll discover a **Meditation Point**. When you reach one of these, it's time to think about and soak in what you've read so far. Then go to the **Study Guide** at the end of the book where you will find questions that will help you remember the main concepts while at the same time give you the opportunity to personalize the concepts and apply them to your own life. To get the fullest benefit from these teachings take time to honestly answer the questions, consider carefully the action steps. You might want to go back through the chapter and circle key points, things you want to know more about, and things you want to remember.

Imagine that you're sitting in your favorite place in the world, enjoying the comfort of familiar surroundings along with the excitement of learning new ideas. This is your study time. God will be there with you, so always ask Him to reveal to you what you should be learning from your reading and study. Learning spiritual things is dynamic, like learning to ride a bike. You can't successfully accomplish the goal by just reading the instruction manual. You must at some point get on the bike and try out what you have read to actually learn and master the material you have read. Learning to grow spiritually is no different so you will want to read and then act on what you have read as you go.

God created it all, so He is the One who can explain it all. Take your time and allow God to speak to you, elaborate on, and make applicable what you have read. You'll soon learn that He has many ways in which He will speak to you. You will hear Him best if you follow the instructions in His Book, written especially to you—the Bible.

You'll also discover **Action and Visualization** instructions throughout this book where I offer a suggested action that could result in a long-term behavioral change. To make these sorts of changes, it's helpful to practice *visualization*. Think of these sections as park benches where you can rest a bit and visualize what you've learned and what that means for your daily life. Take time to consider how you might do things *differently* based on what you have learned.

Let me say a few words about this concept of visualization. God designed your mind with two parts. Your conscious mind is like a computer programmer and your subconscious mind and central nervous system are like the computer itself. If your conscious mind had to deal with all the incoming information and demands for action from every part of the body simultaneously you would be overwhelmed.

Let's use the simple act of driving a car as an example. There are many things you deal with simultaneously while driving. Here are just a few:

- Watch for traffic lights, stop signs, other directional signs in a continually moving landscape.

- Be aware of other cars that are sometimes traveling at speeds near 70 mph.

- Make the correct turns on streets to get to your destination.

- Juggle distractions such as pedestrians, conversations, weather, or radio chatter.

Though your conscious mind can overlap many of these tasks, it is limited to acting on only one at a time. So when you were first learning to drive, you were very conscious of everything going on. As you perform a task once or twice or a few times, you train your subconscious mind—you teach it how to react subconsciously so you can eventually juggle multiple tasks with less demand on the conscious mind. After a few years of driving, you do most of the actions without consciously thinking about them.

Visualization can help program your subconscious mind, too. When you observe something (whether it is something actually happening or even just the idea of this thing pictured in your mind), you begin to program your subconscious how to perform the action. The way our subconscious mind learns is a wonderfully complex system God gave us to help us navigate through life. However, sometimes we use this system to program bad habits.

Once a habit is ingrained in our subconscious, it's difficult to change. Our subconscious mind is trained to respond to cues. When one of these cues appears, our subconscious mind reacts in a specific way before our conscious mind has had a chance to think about or debate the merit of the action. Let's say you're brushing your teeth, but your conscious mind is thinking about what you're going to do today. When you're done squeezing the toothpaste onto your brush, do you automatically put the cap back on the toothpaste? Or are you one of those people who forgets to replace the cap? Visualization can help. It's really as simple as always visualizing ahead of time what you are going to do differently when certain cues appear (like when you finish squeezing the toothpaste tube). If you continually forget to put the cap back on the tube, you would want to take time to picture yourself performing the corrected action and even acting it out. Over time, as you repeat this visualization, you will teach your subconscious to break the old habit.

Well, we're just about ready to unwrap the Gifts of Freedom. But before we do, we'll take one chapter to explore how and why you were created. The subsequent chapters will present the Gifts of Freedom and show you how to unwrap and use them to impact your relationship with God and others. In total, we will unwrap 12 of God's gifts in this book series, ending with an eternal gift—an intimate loving relationship with God Himself.

There is no need to speed through this book. Take the time you need and allow God to interact with you as you consider the biblical truths He presents to you.

Let's get started.

✠ *Every good and perfect gift is from above, coming down from the Father of the heavenly lights, Who does not change like shifting shadows* (James 1:17).

Chapter 1

IN THE BEGINNING...
WHAT'S MY PURPOSE AND WHAT WENT WRONG?

Before you begin to read, pray that the Holy Spirit will give you understanding and application.

✠ *In the beginning God created the heavens and the earth* (Genesis 1:1).

We celebrate beginnings. We have birthdays, anniversaries, national holidays, and grand openings to commemorate these events. Remember the birth of your children or maybe a niece or nephew? How about the first date with your spouse, boyfriend, or girlfriend? Maybe you remember your first kiss? Or how about the day you drove your first car home? These events are powerful and memorable because they are part of your personal history. These "beginnings" helped shape who you are.

There are even greater "beginnings" that shape us, including the beginning of the world and, yes, the beginning of humankind. All of our "beginnings" find their source in God, the Creator of all things, the Giver of all good and perfect gifts.

He is the Giver of life—consciousness, self-awareness, and even the free-will to live life the way you decide to. So what are we to do now? Why are we here? How should we live? What is our purpose? These questions will be answered in this book.

But I'm not grabbing my answers out of thin air—they are collected from the Author of "In the beginning...." God recorded *the beginning* in His words to us, the Bible. Like all good stories, let's start at the beginning. The creation of humankind.

OUR BEGINNING

☩ *Let **Us** make man in our **image**, in our **likeness**...* (Genesis 1:26).

You don't read too far into the first book of the Bible, Genesis, before meeting this foundational verse that answers some of our deepest questions. We were created in the image and likeness of God. If that's true, why are we so messed up? And if we are made in God's image, why are we so inclined to act so ungodly? To answer these questions it is important to learn about God's nature.

Before heading down that path, though, I'd like to clarify something that may be new to you. Do you find it odd that the verse refers to "Us"? Isn't this God's creation story? Yes, it is. The "Us" in this verse is indeed God. But God is also known as the Holy Trinity (God: the Father, the Son [Jesus], and the Holy Spirit)—three-in-one. God's use of "Us" here says that all three were present *in the beginning*.

So, what does that mean for you personally? You were originally designed to be created in God's *image*—according to His *likeness*. Let's take a closer look at the words *image* and *likeness*. These words are used in tandem to clarify an overall meaning. *Image* is translated from the Hebrew word *tselem* which means "a reproductive or duplicative form of a person or object like a statue." This suggests we were created to resemble God in form or appearance. Obviously this doesn't refer to our physical composition so it would have to relate to spirit and character. Balancing this is the word *likeness*. This word comes from the Hebrew word *demut* which does not convey such preciseness as image. To be "like" someone means "you possess many, but not all of the characteristics and qualities."[1]

So what, then, does it mean to be created in God's image and likeness? We must first ask some questions about God. What is His composition? What is His character? What is His nature? Then we can determine in what ways we are like Him or were *intended* to be like Him.

You've probably seen paintings or illustrations depicting God as an old man with a long, white flowing beard. This is a common approach artists take in their attempts to give God a "face." I imagine the image of an old white-bearded man is often chosen because it conjures up a picture of wisdom and, if you have ever read *The Lord of the Rings* (think of Gandalf), of mystical power as well. But I'm sure you already know that God is not a human being with a body, head, two arms, and two legs. He is something indefinable and, for lack of a better word, invisible. So now what? How can we learn about Someone we can't see? The Bible says one way we can better understand God is to examine some of His work:

God has made it plain to them [humankind]. *For since the creation of the world God's invisible qualities—His eternal power and divine nature—have been **clearly seen, being understood** from what has been **made**, so that men are without excuse* (Romans 1:19-20).

Hmm...the verse says we will be without excuse if we don't examine God's work, so let's examine it carefully.

GOD IS LIGHT

Take a look at the first thing God creates, as recorded in Genesis:

✠ *And God said, "Let there be light," and there was light* (Genesis 1:3).

What is light? Light is energy. Light rays move at 186,282.397 miles per *second* (over 670 *million* miles per hour). That's a speed we really can't comprehend. Albert Einstein's special theory of relativity ($E=mc^2$) states that the speed of light is the same for all observers, even if they are in motion at different speed relative to one another.[2] Read that again if you need to. Got it? That is significant because the speed of light is not just the velocity of "light" but also a fundamental feature of the way space and time are tied together. God created light—and He is the same to everybody, no matter what race they are, what language they speak, what status they have, or what they have done; He is the fundamental core tying everything together.

I once heard a lecture by a Christian physicist who offered this interesting proposition, which is based on Einstein's theory and carefully selected Bible verses: God's essence is light, and if you were to travel the speed of light you would enter the dimension of Heaven. The physicist was very persuasive, but whether or not his theory has any merit, I believe we can learn a lot about God's attributes and nature by looking at God's first creation—light. God is certainly like light. We'll discover that this theme is significant to God's story, and to our understanding of what it means to follow Him.

When we "see" something, anything, our eyes are actually detecting light rays either coming from an object (such as the sun) or reflecting off an object (like the moon). So without light we *can not* see anything at all. Similarly, without God we *can not* see or experience the spiritual things of this life. The Bible says:

✠ *For with You* [God] *is the fountain of life; in Your light we see light* (Psalm 36:9).

✠ *The commands of the Lord are radiant, giving light to the eyes* (Psalm 19:8).

✠ *Blessed are those who have learned to acclaim You, who walk in the light of Your presence, O Lord* (Psalm 89:15).

✠ *In Him* [Jesus] *was life, and that life was the light of men* (John 1:4).

The sign signifying Jesus entering into our world was a bright *light* in the sky and Jesus Himself says:

✠ *I am the Light of the world. Whoever follows Me will never walk in darkness, but will have the light of life* (John 8:12).

The Bible describes those who have become Christians in this way:

✠ *For you were once darkness, but now you are light in the Lord. Live as children of light* (Ephesians 5:8).

God uses "light" to identify Himself so we can better understand His nature. I have counted over 70 times in the Bible where He uses this analogy. Because you know the properties of light, you will better understand Him. His light is necessary for spiritual sight or *insight*. This is why I suggest that at the beginning of each chapter (or whenever you pick up the book) you pray for better understanding before you start reading—so your insight will be *improved*.

WHO BROUGHT EVIL INTO THE WORLD?

Let's consider another aspect of God's nature by looking at good and evil. Simply put, *good* is what God wills and *evil* is that which is outside the will of God. Evil therefore can *not* come from God. For instance, light cannot create darkness; its mere presence negates or *illuminates* darkness. Darkness only exists where light is *not* present. His will (good) negates that which is not His will (evil). The Bible says it succinctly:

✝ *...the Lord is good...* (Psalm 34:8).

✝ *...God is light; in Him there is no darkness at all* (1 John 1:5).

People often ask this question: "If God is so good, then why is there so much evil and pain in the world?" It is a great question. And the answer begins with understanding this truth about God's nature—that there is no darkness (or evil) in Him; He could not create any evil (light cannot create darkness).

✝ *For everything God created is good...* (1 Timothy 4:4).

So where does evil come from? Well, we live in a broken world with broken people who are not acting according to God's will—in His image and likeness. We substantially removed God from ourselves and our world as you will come to understand from this review of our biblical history (the

Fall of humankind)—and that very absence is why and where evil exists. In other words, the absence of light (God's image and likeness) shinning through us into the world allows the darkness to exist. We were created to bring His very light (image and likeness) into the world—to *light* the world which humankind collectively decided *not* to do. So it's important to understand that the responsibility for this broken world and people is ours.

God gave us a wonderful gift—freedom of choice. However, it is a two-edged sword, and with one edge we have sliced open the curtain that brought evil into this world. But there is good news—the other edge of the sword still works. God invites us to choose the side that leads to Him.

There is a scientific theory on the structure of the universe that says if you aimed yourself in any direction and rocketed that way past all the stars and other galaxies, you would eventually come back to yourself, the original starting point. Since we can't actually do this, it will always remain, like so much of science, just a theory (though a very popular theory). Our spiritual lives are similar—the responsibility for the choices we make comes back to us. The Law of Cause and Effect says: every choice has consequences. We suffer or enjoy the consequences of all the choices we make individually and corporately.

GOD IS SPIRIT

It says in the Bible that God is a spirit being:

☩ *God is spirit...* (John 4:24).

Hmm…but we're not spirit beings are we? We have a physical presence. Does that mean we aren't created in the image and likeness of God after all? No. But it does suggest that Adam, the first man, was created different from us, and something changed since creation so we are not the same as Adam.

You will see how we are born into one stage, and through our lives here on earth, are afforded the opportunity (by our choice) to move toward what God intended us to be—someone made in His image and likeness. If this is a process, a "moving toward" something, then when are we actually finished being made, and what will we be upon completion?

Here again God has given clues in His creation that help us understand how such a miraculous change—a metamorphosis—can occur. Consider the butterfly. It begins life as a fertilized egg, then becomes a small baby caterpillar, then grows into an adult caterpillar, then forms itself in a cocoon, then goes through a reconfiguring process, and *only* after emerging from that cocoon, does it achieve its ultimate purpose—a butterfly full of beauty and fluttering flight. The butterfly has periods of gradual development and also times of dramatic change. If you look at the creature in any one of its pre-butterfly stages you might not believe it could possibly reach the destiny for which God created it.

The same is true for us. God gave His creation, you and me, the gifts of growth and metamorphosis. We, like the butterfly, face transition points that may be gradual or quite dramatic. There is even a kind of death, not unlike the cocoon stage that immediately precedes a person's emergence as a complete and beautiful new creature. Growth isn't always easy. It may seem impossible to fully appreciate or even believe what God's ultimate purpose is for us during any given step of the process. I doubt you could convince a caterpillar that one day it would fly. And yet, God had a plan and purpose for it. God has a plan and purpose for you, too.

It's interesting to note that butterflies truly have to struggle to get out of their cocoons but that very struggle actually helps the butterfly prepare for flight in the new world. I believe the same is true for us as we work through each stage in our development to become people who reflect or imbue God's image and likeness. Each trial, challenge, and difficulty we experience can better prepare us for the next stage of our development.

When we look at Adam, the first man, we see a man who definitely was created in the image and likeness of God. We can also see how his choice (and Eve's) caused humankind to take a *big* step backward in that regard. (A full examination of Adam and Eve's poor choices are found later in this chapter.) And unfortunately after the Fall, they could only pass down to us (their children) what they possessed—a form less than God originally intended.

You might think it would be "game over" for us at this point—how can we ever find our way back to God's original design? But God already had a plan based on our own failure and free will—one that offers every man and woman the potential to become whole, to become the person He intended and desires us to be. We, the sons and daughters of Adam and Eve, *all* begin life as *less* than God intended. We are in a continual growth process, striving to change into the image and likeness of God. The exact nature of your spiritual growth and stages of your metamorphosis you will understand as we discover what the Bible says about you.

Let's get back to God's composition, to find our target as we aim toward growth.

✟ *God is **spirit** and His worshipers must worship in **spirit** and in truth* (John 4:24).

God is spirit, or a spirit being. But there's more—in this verse we also learn that we must have a spirit with which to worship Him, or, in essence *communicate* with Him. From this, we can deduce that God intended at least some part of us to be *spirit* and this spiritual component plays a significant role in how God wants to communicate with us.

✟ *Don't you know that you yourselves are God's temple and that God's **Spirit** lives in you?* (1 Corinthians 3:16)

✟ *...he who unites himself with the Lord is one with Him **in spirit*** (1 Corinthians 6:17).

It seems that God intended us to *be* spirit beings *with* a mind *in* a body. We were also made in such a way that God's Spirit and our spirit can be *connected—united*. For Adam, the first man, his spirit was connected with God's Spirit from "day one" giving him 20/20 (perfect) insight. However, after Adam's sin, the connection changed. We no longer had, by default, a perfect connection between our spirit and God's. But there is good news: God has made a path to redeem that broken connection. God offers a gift that can lead us back, back to a functioning relationship between our spirit and His. What other attributes or characteristics of God might we receive from this functioning connection with God's Spirit?

GOD IS LOVE

The apostle John wrote with simplicity and eloquence:

✟ *...God is **love*** (1 John 4:8).

Of course, that word *love* can mean different things to different people. The Bible offers this definition:

✟ ***Love** is patient, **love** is kind. It does not envy, it does not boast, it is not proud. It is not rude, it is not self-seeking, it is not easily angered, it keeps no record of wrongs. **Love** does not delight in evil but rejoices with the truth. It always protects, always trust, always hopes, always perseveres* (1 Corinthians 13:4-7).

You only have to read the morning newspaper to see how God's creation, humankind, is missing the mark regarding love. Violence, war, terrorism, and countless other evils are clearly the result of people who are *not* living out the biblical definition of love. Each one of us has fallen short of living out this biblical definition at one time or another. But God desires us to reach for and regain His character of love. Thankfully, God also desires to help us get there.

How did we get so far off track from what we were intended to be? Well, in alignment with His desire for us to be in His image and His desire to have an authentic loving relationship with us, God gave us a free will—our own free will with which we could make our *own* decisions. This is the mechanism which allows us to show love. God could have created a companion without a free will. Perhaps a sock puppet.

God: "What are you going to do today puppet?"

God's "sock puppet" voice: "Whatever you make me do, God."

Can a sock puppet love its owner? No. But if it had the ability to choose, then, yes, it could love—with its own free will. However, it could also choose *not* to love. This is an interesting dynamic that is crucial to understanding free will, and understanding who is bringing evil into the world.

Adam and Eve had a choice: to follow God or not. They decided to disobey God. With this same free will we can decide to follow God—to pursue the path to becoming more like God's original creation. We can decide if we want to be companions with God. We can also decide how *much* of a companion we want to be. Using my earlier analogy, we can choose to move from being an egg to a caterpillar or a caterpillar to a butterfly. We can even decide if we want to grow at all. We are responsible for our own spiritual growth. As the process unfolds in these pages, you'll discover that while God gives us the means, *we* have to *choose* to go through the *process*.

Right now you may be thinking there is no way to get from here to there, from the person you are today to someone who reflects the *image* and *likeness* of *God*. However, the Bible gives us a clear way to pursue this goal, showing us how to receive, unwrap, and use the Gifts of Freedom.

To start walking down that pathway we need to recover an active spirit that God can connect with. This is what happens when we accept the first gift. From there, we begin a slow growth process to developing God's character of *Love*. After we die, we'll be judged by Him based on our decision to follow that path, and how we followed it:

✟ *Just as man is destined to die once, and after that to face judgment...* (Hebrews 9:27).

That may sound a bit daunting, but there is good news for those who have chosen the path to follow God. He loves us so much that He provided a way for His followers to be freed from this judgment, to receive new glorious bodies like the butterflies do that allow them to fly in freedom.

✟ *But our citizenship* [those who accept the first gift] *is in Heaven. And we eagerly await a Savior from there, the Lord Jesus Christ, Who, by the power that enables Him to bring everything under His control, will **transform** our lowly bodies so that they will be **like His glorious body*** (Philippians 3:20-21).

This major decision will impact the rest of your life—and determine what happens at the *end* of that life. Choosing to follow God will dramatically change you. Not only will that choice give you the gift of eternal life, but your life in the here-and-now will be completely different. You will be unrecognizable from who you once were by *choosing* growth. But if you refuse to follow God, you will miss having a connection to God that allows you to reach your potential of being able to fully exude His kind of love.

WHAT WENT WRONG

When Adam and Eve made the decision not to follow God's instruction, their relationship with Him was drastically altered. Let's start at the beginning and see what happened.

Just as God the Father, Jesus, and the Holy Spirit have always been in relationship with each other, they (the Trinity) desired the same for Adam.

☩ *The Lord God said, "It is not good for the man to be alone. I will make a helper suitable for him"* (Genesis 2:18).

☩ *So the Lord God caused the man to fall into a deep sleep; and while he was sleeping, He took one of the man's ribs and closed up the place with flesh. Then the Lord God made a woman from the rib He had taken out of man and brought her to the man* (Genesis 2:21-22).

We see in this passage that women were also created in God's image and meant to exude His character.

☩ *The man and his wife were both naked, and they felt no shame* (Genesis 2:25).

Adam and Eve were originally created with a physical presence and a mind that could freely choose what to do and how to act; however, Adam and Eve also had a spiritual aspect that connected them with God. God's love flowed in and through them so they would reflect and shine God's light into His creation. We were originally created in the image and likeness of God in *composition, self-determination,* and *character.*

It is significant that Adam and Eve were naked and yet had no shame. This tells me that God's Spirit was shining through them and with God's shinning Spirit *covering* them they had no reason to feel any shame—even without clothes. I like to explain it this way. Adam and Eve's bodies were like glass light bulbs. The light itself is God's light coming into us through His Spirit and ours then radiating out of us to exude His image and likeness. When a light bulb is lit, you don't really notice the bulb itself. However, you *do* notice (and desire) the light. God's character and glory shining through us is to be the essence of our real beauty. I don't want to minimize the importance of our own spirit—God created each of us as unique individuals. But when our spirit and God's Spirit combined in the original design, I believe the light was so strong that it overshadowed the physical body—the glass bulb. Our purpose is not merely to exist or to physically look good (about which many people today have so much anxiety); our purpose is to shine His light, represent God in His creation, and to shine His glory into it.

✠ *...he* [man] *is the image and glory of God...* (1 Corinthians 11:7).

✠ *...subdue it* [the earth]. *Rule over the fish of the sea and the birds of the air and over every living creature that moves on the ground* (Genesis 1:28).

Adam and Eve had nothing to be ashamed of because God's character was exuding from them. To shine with God's love and in His love is to truly feel no shame. Clearly they were given the responsibility and the authority on earth to execute that responsibility. Understanding that we are given authority over the creation *along with* free will is critical to understanding why there is now so much evil in the world in spite of God's character of love.

We are *not* created to be robots or clones. Moreover, God creates each of us as a unique light bulb—a person with a unique mind and personality. So when we're connected with Him as Adam and Eve were in the Garden, His light shines through our unique personalities, creating diverse patterns, like light shining through crystals.

Let's get back to the Garden. Adam and Eve were living in a paradise garden home, they had full communion with God and reflected His glory into His creation. God had given them certain clear instructions about how to enjoy and interact with His creation.

✟ *Now the Lord God had planted a garden in the east, in Eden; and there he put the man he had formed...And the Lord God commanded the man, "You are free to eat from any tree in the garden; but you must not eat from the tree of the knowledge of good and evil, for when you eat of it you will surely die"* (Genesis 2:8,16-17).

I like to think of the Garden of Eden as one of those amusement parks enjoyed by children (and childlike parents). Remember the Ferris wheel? What a great ride. As it slowly revolves taking you high into the air, it gives you both a sense of exhilaration and a wonderful view of the surrounding area. But imagine if you put your hand into the Ferris wheel's machinery—you'd be seriously injured, perhaps even killed. God created a wonderful place for man to enjoy filled with amazing things to see and experience, but He also gave Adam a safety rule to follow so he could enjoy the garden without risk of harm—don't eat of the fruit of the tree of knowledge. Sounds simple enough, right? And for a while, it probably was. God must have loved it when Adam communicated his enjoyment of the Garden with Him and shone His light into the world.

Then satan entered the picture. Satan was an angel who once led worship over God's throne, but he developed pride in his beauty and his abilities–desiring to steal God's glory for himself. For this, he was cast from Heaven:

✠ *All your pomp has been brought down to the grave* [meaning death as in separation from God], *along with the noise of your harps...How you have fallen from Heaven, O morning star, son of the dawn! You have been cast down to the earth, you who once laid low the nations! You said in your heart, "I will ascend to Heaven; I will raise my throne above the stars of God...I will make myself like the Most High"* (Isaiah 14:11-14).

Satan's mistake was in putting *his* will above God's will and considering himself more important than God. As a result he fell from Heaven—he was separated from God. We will discuss satan's role in a later chapter, but this is important to know right now—misery loves company. Satan was jealous and fearful of man reflecting God's image into the world. He wanted Adam and Eve to join him in putting their wills and desires above God's, so he approached Eve:

✠ *...He* [satan] *said to the woman, "Did God really say, 'you must not eat from any tree in the garden'?" The woman said to the serpent* [satan], *"We may eat fruit from the trees in the garden, but God did say 'You must not eat fruit from the tree that is in the middle of the garden, and you must not touch it or you will die.'" "You will not surely die" the serpent said to the woman. "For God knows that when you eat of it your eyes will be opened, and you will be like God, knowing good and evil"* (Genesis 3:1-5).

Remember that free will God gave Adam and Eve (and us)? Satan decided to tempt Eve to use her free will—to become as God, just like he had tried to do. Instead of listening to the Spirit of God in her, she was influenced by her senses; and her desires caused her mind to make the wrong choice:

✠ *When the woman saw that the fruit of the tree was good for food and pleasing to the eye, and also desirable for gaining wisdom, she took some and ate it. She also gave some to her husband, who was with her, and he ate it* (Genesis 3:6).

Adam and Eve wanted more than just to reflect God's image and likeness—they wanted to become "gods." By rejecting God's instruction, Adam and Eve broke communion with God. Many people in today's world also want to set their *own* rules and *be* their own god—they freely choose to disobey *God's will* and subsequently suffer the consequences of a life without taking direction from their Creator.

SPIRITUAL DEATH

Since God is the source of spiritual life in us, Adam and Eve's spirits became functionally dead and their glory, gone. This immediate separation from God's Spirit as a result of sin eventually resulted in physical death for Adam and Eve. Spiritual and ultimately physical death then spread into the world, tainting humanity by multiplying Adam and Eve's sin from that day forward:

✠ *Therefore, just as sin entered the world through one man, and death through sin, and in this way death came to all men, because all sinned* (Romans 5:12).

✠ *Jesus replied, "I tell you the truth, everyone who sins is a slave to sin"* (John 8:34).

The Bible says our slavery will exist until we receive the knowledge of truth and then *act* on it to escape.

☩ *...leading them* [you] *to a knowledge of the truth, and that they* [you] *will come to their* [your] *senses and escape from the trap of the devil, who has taken them* [you] *captive to do his will* (2 Timothy 2:25-26).

Continuing on with Adam and Eve's story, they knew right away things had *changed*:

☩ *Then the eyes of both of them were opened, and they realized they were naked; so they sewed fig leaves together and made coverings for themselves* (Genesis 3:7).

There are three things I'd like to point out from this passage of Scripture. The first thing to note is that the "eyes of both of them were *opened*" meaning they had lost their insight (spiritual sight) and now had to un-naturally rely *only* on their physical eyes for sight. Their vision became distorted and solely physical.

Second, have you ever wondered why scientists say we only use such a small fraction of our brain capacity and power? Perhaps it's because we were designed to have substantially more information coming in through our spirits which needed to be processed and integrated into our daily activities.

Third, with their *spirit* disconnected, the *glory* was gone. Using my light bulb analogy—the light went out. I believe until you are "born again"— until you accept Christ as your personal Savior—the light *Source* is unavailable. After you are born again, the light Source is always within reach, but only dimly as we develop this new connection (our intimate relationship with God), and then of course only to the degree we turn it up (become more like Him). As we become closer to His image and likeness, closer to Him, our light brightens. The light does not reach its full potential until we're in Heaven with new bodies, when we will truly be in an intimate relationship and then shine fully in the image and likeness of God.

I do not suggest that God's love is not currently being manifested even by those who have not re-hooked up to the Source. God's invisible qualities, including His divine nature, are evident in the world for all to see. However, since the fall we have been infected with sin and self-absorption which distorts His love. Unfortunately, many times when people experience each other they may only experience the sin and self-absorption that has grown rampant since the Fall.

There may be faint moments when they experience God's love shinning through, but this low intensity light is merely a reflection or residue. If people are not hooked up to the Source the light will not be of full quality or intensity that God designed us to shine. The good news: God can plug us in again and the light can flow again to bring healing to those areas in our lives affected by sin.

It is a requirement that you start this healing process before you die so you can assure your entrance into Heaven. This reconnection is necessary because for Heaven to be the kind of experience for me that God promises, you and others there have to be exuding His *full* light. There can be no sin or disharmony in Heaven or there can be no true heavenly experience. This is an important point: for us to spend eternity in the kind of Heaven God desires us to, we all inherently have to be the kind of beings He desires us to be—He leaves the choice to become that person up to each of us. Upon agreeing to become a heavenly being we can enter and become part of that wonderful experience.

So after Adam and Eve fell, sin entered the world and their primary communication method was no longer a spiritual one, but physical. Their physical eyes were open and the world as they knew it was not quite so wonderful anymore. They saw the raw weakness of themselves. They must have felt very insecure once they'd lost their main focus—their connection with God. From that moment forward, they would judge themselves and each other, for the first time *fully conscious* of the difference between *good* and *evil*.

God's *glory* had been the primary source of their beauty and strength; without it they became ashamed of what they saw—that new evil side, the opposite of God's will. Realizing their own frailty, they covered their bodies with fig leaves in an effort to cover their sin and insecurity. This may have given them some comfort; however, we will see later that it was not adequate covering for God. Fig leaves and clothes and even an appearance of doing the right things aren't enough to hide sin from God.

✠ *Then the man and his wife heard the sound of the Lord God as He was walking in the garden in the cool of the day, and they hid from the Lord God among the trees of the garden* (Genesis 3:8).

There is a lot of important information in this one verse. First, God walked with man in the garden. His relationship with Adam and Eve was one of close community. So when they realized their sin, they tried to hide from God. I can imagine them thinking, "Maybe if He doesn't see us, He won't notice our sin." But this would have been only half of the story, because they also feared God. They feared Him because they knew what they had done was wrong. Without that internal connection, the spirit to *Spirit* connection, God must have seemed frighteningly different.

GOD REACHES OUT TO US

I like this next verse. It seems almost comical at first, but the significance behind the words is profound.

✠ *But the Lord God called to the man, "Where are you?"* (Genesis 3:9).

God knew where Adam and Eve were. But this verse tells us several more things about God. First, it was natural for God to speak to Adam and Eve in the garden. This says something about God's character—He is relational and He desires communication—and that communication should feel as natural as our human-to-human relationships. It also shows us that God desires us to be honest with Him. And finally, it tells us that God wants, *not* for His sake but for each of our own, for us to answer the question—"Where are you?" Adam answered God this way:

✟ *He [Adam] answered, "I heard you in the garden, and I was afraid because I was naked; so I hid"* (Genesis 3:10).

Adam didn't know he was naked—it wasn't unusual—until he'd sinned. But recognizing that sin (and the fact that the light had gone out—the glory was gone), he desperately wanted to hide from God, knowing God would see his raw self, without God's good light covering him.

Many people today do the same thing; when they recognize they are outside of God's will they want to hide from Him. Maybe you too right now relate to Adam's answer. I believe many people never come to know God because they are afraid of Him. They don't feel they are worthy to have a relationship with their Creator. They believe their sin is too great. As we explore the Bible, you'll find nothing is further from the truth! No matter what you have done or where you are–God is calling you to receive His unconditional love. There are no sins too large or numerous that God can't forgive.

The story goes on:

✟ *And He said, "Who told you that you were naked? Have you eaten from the tree that I commanded you not to eat from?" The man said, "The woman you put here with me—she gave me some fruit from the tree, and I ate it." Then the Lord God said to the woman, "What is this you have done?" The woman said, "The serpent deceived me, and I ate"* (Genesis 3:11-13).

When God asked Adam what happened, Adam did not take responsibility for his actions. He blamed the woman, and then also blamed God because God gave him the woman. Eve blamed the snake. They both claimed to be victims. You may be familiar with this type of behavior or reaction. Obviously, Adam and Eve's newly-discovered victim mentality is *not* a character trait found in the *image* and *likeness* of God.

While we know Adam and Eve went on after "the fall" to physically populate the world, they did so with the full weight of sin on their shoulders—and the result of that sin was eventual physical death to coincide with their newly acquired spiritual death.

✠ *And the Lord God said, "The man has now become like one of us* [as a result of eating from the tree of knowledge], *knowing good and evil. He must not be allowed to reach out his hand and take also from the tree of life and eat, and live forever." So the Lord God banished him from the Garden of Eden to work the ground from which he had been taken"* (Genesis 3:22-23).

The banishment from the Garden of Eden (where Adam and Eve were now unable to eat from the Tree of Life which is now available to us in Jesus Christ) proclaims their physical death sentence. However, this physical death was not the most important issue to God—it was the loss of relationship and spiritual connection with the ones He created in His own image.

As the body without the spirit is dead... (James 2:26).

God intended for us to be made up of three working parts as the apostle Paul outlined to the Christians at Thessalonica.

✠ *May your whole **spirit, soul,** and **body** be kept blameless at the* [second] *coming of our Lord, Jesus Christ* (1 Thessalonians 5:23).

The soul, or what I refer to as the "mind," consists of your intellect, emotions, and will. When you become a Christian, your mind, along with your body and your newly-functioning spirit, are bound together as one. It is your will (computer programmer) that decides your course by balancing the input from your intellect, emotions, and bodily desires against that of your spirit's input from God.

God's priority is our spiritual side, not the physical fulfillment and obsession with our bodies' needs—which often become *our* primary focus. Fun, pleasure and comfort are all temporal things, but the spirit is an eternal thing. It's no wonder our minds make physical pleasure and comfort a main priority because our minds are overwhelmed with information coming through our body's senses. This can distort our view of reality (both spiritual and physical as well as their relationship to each other) and our sin, then further distorts our perception of reality.

DISTORTED REALITY

Allow me, for just a moment, to illustrate this skewed perspective that comes from focusing on the importance of our physical being. Have you noticed that we rate sin by its impact on our physical bodies? A little white lie is not as bad as theft, and theft not as bad as assault, and assault is not as bad as murder. Even in our attempts to understand sin, we end up focusing on how our bodies are affected.

However, God is more concerned about how your spirit and your relationship with Him is affected. *All* sin causes you to be out of God's will and therefore equally affects your relationship.

✠ *For whoever keeps the whole law and yet stumbles at just one point is guilty of breaking all of it* (James 2:10).

You are going to see as we dig deeper and deeper into God's Word that as we do God's will (exude His light) versus our own, we will have better spiritual clarity and understanding.

When we view the world only through our physical senses and the demands of our bodies, it is like viewing the world through a prism. The picture is distorted. Sin distorts it even further. Some people turn the sin prism into a kaleidoscope, which may be colorful and compelling to look through, but it also makes it impossible to gain even a reasonable perspective of spiritual realities. I want to clarify that nobody has a perfect perspective, because no one, except Jesus, lives in complete obedience. However, our goal (and the very purpose of this book) should be to find every possible way to improve our perspective and act on that perception.

You see it is with our physical senses that we detect, and then with our minds to understand physical truth (which is temporal); however, it is through our spirit's insight that we see and understand spiritual truth (which is eternal). What's important to understand is that Truth (with a capital T) will eventually and always trump truth (small t). After we get linked back up to God's light, we have the power with our free will to start developing this insight no matter what prisms or kaleidoscopes we currently look through. This will allow you to then see the reality that really matters the most to you.

GOD OF JUSTICE AND MERCY

The Bible repeatedly identifies God as a just God. Because of this, sins must be punished or there is no justice at all. Imagine if judges routinely did not enforce the law! Chaos would be the result. A world without true justice is cruel to its occupants. Also, there can be no love without justice. If you saw someone you love doing something hurtful to themselves, wouldn't your attempt to correct the person be an act of love? Love demands that we correct others when they do wrong. God is indeed a God of love, which makes Him also a God of justice.

✝ *...the Lord disciplines those He loves, as a father the son He delights in* (Proverbs 3:12).

✝ *...Yes, Lord God Almighty,* **true** *and* **just** *are your judgments* (Revelations 16:7).

God desires and created us to live in a Heaven-like environment. Because of the Fall, we, like Adam and Eve, live in a world full of evil and pain. When we do finally get to Heaven we will have established a complete record of evidence on our own failure to live life without Him as He had warned us of in the beginning.

✝ *...I have set before you life and death, blessing and curses. Now* **choose life**, *so that you and your children may live and that you may love the Lord your God,* **listen** *to his voice and* **hold fast to Him**... (Deuteronomy 30:19-20).

In spite of our failures our Father in Heaven loves and wants an eternal relationship with us—for us to *hold fast* to Him. Out of love for us, God did *not* want sin, along with the negative effects of sin (rudeness, violence, wars, terrorism, etc.) to last for an *eternity*, therefore sin must result in *death* so it can be extinguished once and for all. At the same time, He created a way for sin to be punished without condemning *us* all to *eternal* death. He did this by sending His son, an *innocent man*, who agreed to take our punishment so that both justice and love would be fulfilled. His innocent blood shed on the Cross covers our sin in the sight of God so that when God sees us, God sees Christ's righteousness. Though this story is described in the New Testament, the need for our sins to be covered by the shedding of innocent blood was foreshadowed back in Genesis:

✠ *The Lord God made garments of skin for Adam and his wife and clothed them* (Genesis 3:21).

God took their fig leaves and replaced them with animal skins. He shed the blood of innocent animals to cover Adam and Eve's sins. This became a familiar practice for the Jews in the Old Testament; offering animal sacrifices to cover their sins. However, they had to continually offer sacrifices because their sacrifices were not perfect or permanent. Jesus Christ became the perfect, final, and complete sacrifice.

✠ *In Him* [Jesus Christ] *we have redemption through His blood, the forgiveness of sins, in accordance with the riches of God's grace...*(Ephesians 1:7).

✠ *...To Him* [Jesus Christ] *who loves us and has freed us from our sins by His blood...* (Revelation 1:6).

✝ *...For He* [Jesus Christ] *has clothed me with garments of salvation and arrayed me in a robe of righteousness* [right standing with God]*...* (Isaiah 61:10).

It is *only* by Jesus' sacrifice that we could re-enter an eternal intimate relationship with God. When we die this *eternal relationship* brings us into and indeed is that experience we call *Heaven*. Jesus described eternal life this way.

✝ [Jesus said] *"Now this is **eternal life**: that they [you and me] may **know You** the only true God, and Jesus Christ whom You have sent"* (John 17:3).

Hell can simply be defined as an eternity without accepting Christ's reconciliation of an eternal relationship with God.

✝ *Remember that at that time you were separated from Christ, excluded from citizenship in Israel [Heaven] and foreigners to the covenants of the promise, without hope and without God in the world. But now in Christ Jesus you once were far away and have been brought near through the blood of Christ. For He Himself is our peace, Who has made the two one and has destroyed the barrier, the dividing wall of hostility, by abolishing in His flesh the law with its commandments and regulations. His purpose was to create in Himself one new man out of two thus making peace, and in this one body to reconcile both of them to God through the cross, by which He put to death their hostility.... For through Him we both have **access** to the Father by one Spirit. Consequently, you are no longer foreigners and aliens, but **fellow citizens with God's people and members of God's household*** (Ephesians 2:12-19).

It is also through Jesus Christ that we eventually get back our glory:

✟ *When Christ, who is your life, appears, then you will also appear with Him in glory* (Colossians 3:4).

By reconnecting with God's Spirit, we can be transformed by God into His image and likeness as He originally intended, receiving freedom from the restrictions that kept us from obtaining this glory, a glory we can, to some degree, obtain here and now in this life:

✟ *Now the Lord is the Spirit and where the Spirit of the Lord is, there is freedom. And we, who with unveiled faces all reflect the Lord's glory, are being transformed into His likeness with **ever-increasing** glory, which comes from the Lord, who is the Spirit* (2 Corinthians 3:17-18).

Jesus Christ is the key to reconnecting with God's Spirit and freeing you from the effects of sin in your life. The process begins with a decision to receive, unwrap, and use the Gifts of Freedom God offers. Let's unwrap the first gift.

MEDITATION POINT

Jesus brings life to you.

Go to Chapter 1 in the Study Guide section on page 269.

ENDNOTES

1   *The Broadman Bible Commentary, Vol. 1* (Nashville, TN: Broadman Press, 1973), 24-25.

2   "Theory of Relativity" Encyclopedia Britannica. 2008. Encyclopedia Britannica Online. Retrieved February 18, 2008, from http://www.britannica.com/eb/article-9109465.

Chapter 2

Gift #1—Life (Part 1)
How do you get it?

Before you begin to read, pray that the Holy Spirit
will give you understanding and application.

✝ *For the wages of sin is death, but the **gift** of God is eternal life in
Christ Jesus our Lord* (Romans 6:23).

✝ *For it is by grace you have been saved, through faith—and this not
from yourselves, it is the **gift** of God—not by works, so that no one
can boast* (Ephesians 2:8-9).

D o you remember what it felt like as a child to wake up on Christmas
day and race from your bedroom to discover presents under the
tree? Anticipation and excitement swirled inside you at a dizzying
pace as you reached for each gift with your name on it. Were you a careful
unwrapper? Or did you tear into the paper with wild excitement? The Bible
says that the first *gift* God offers us is eternal life, accepted through faith
alone. Eternal life would be a pretty big Christmas gift to open by anyone's
standard!

Remember your childlike wonder on Christmas Day—the waiting, the expectancy—the genuine expression of surprise and delight? Jesus loves that childlike wonder and excitement—that genuine expression of surprise and delight. In fact, when asked who was the greatest in Heaven, Jesus answered:

✟ *I tell you the truth, unless you* **change** *and* **become** *like little children, you will never enter the Kingdom of Heaven. Therefore, whoever humbles himself like this child is the greatest in the Kingdom of Heaven* (Matthew 18:3-4).

He wants us to keep this childlike nature as we get to know Him and unwrap His gifts because children have an open, accepting, non-critical, and trusting attitude. Having this attitude should be easy as God's gifts are so wonderful and are available year-round. The question is: will you receive, unwrap, and use them?

THE GIFT OF SALVATION

The first gift is the most important. It has an "open this first" sticker on it because it's a prerequisite for all the other gifts. I'm referring to the gift of salvation. God clearly offers this gift to all of us, but the nature of gift-giving is that you can't receive a gift you refuse to accept. And, it's impossible to receive a gift by force. God does not force us to become His companions. Remember, God gives us free choice in this process of reconciliation and relationship. Jesus talks about this first step of salvation with Nicodemus, a religious ruler. Let's read the exchange they had:

☩ *He* [Nicodemus] *came to Jesus at night and said, "Rabbi, we know you are a teacher who has come from God. For no one could perform the miraculous signs you are doing if God were not with him." In reply Jesus declared, "I tell you the truth, no one can see the kingdom of God unless he is born again." "How can a man be born when he is old?" Nicodemus asked. "Surely he cannot enter a second time into his mother's womb to be born!" Jesus answered, "I tell you the truth, no one can enter the kingdom of God unless he is born of water and the Spirit* [human]. *Flesh gives birth to flesh, but the* [God's] **Spirit gives birth to spirit.** *You should not be surprised at my saying, "You must be **born again**"* (John 3:2-7).

Nicodemus was confused and surprised because it was not an answer he expected. Born again? Of course Jesus was not speaking physically. He was speaking about the rebirth of our spirit. Jesus essentially tells Nicodemus that his spirit isn't capable of connecting with God's Spirit without rebirth. He says, in essence, that while our mother gives us physical life at birth (flesh births flesh), *only God* can give us this spiritual life (Spirit births spirit). Jesus tells Nicodemus that if he wishes to experience the Kingdom of God, he needs a fully operational spirit—a spirit that connects with God the way He intended.

Jesus goes on to describe how to experience this rebirth:

☩ *...that everyone who believes in Him* [Jesus] *may have eternal life. For God so loved the world that He gave His one and only Son, that whoever believes in Him shall not perish but have eternal life* (John 3:15-16).

When Jesus speaks of eternal life, He is speaking about both our physical and spiritual lives. Those who believe in Jesus will receive reborn spirits now, as well as glorious new bodies in Heaven where they will be in an intimate relationship with God for eternity.

✛ *...[Jesus Christ] who, by the power that enables Him to bring everything under His control will transform our lowly bodies so they will be like His glorious body* (Philippians 3:21).

✛ [Jesus said] *"Now this is eternal life: that they may know You, the only true God, and Jesus Christ, whom You have sent"* (John 17:3).

What happens to those who don't choose to believe in Jesus? They have an eternal destiny, too, though one separate from God. The Bible refers to this as hell.

✛ *The wicked shall be turned into hell, and all the nations that forget God* (Psalm 9:17 NKJV).

It's important to note what is meant by the word *wicked* here. In the simplest of terms, a wicked person is someone who does evil—or someone who does the opposite of God's will. But none of us is perfect. We all fail. If we factor in what Jesus says to Nicodemus, we can see that it's not only individual actions against God's will that send someone to hell—eternity without God's presence—it is ultimately the decision to deny God. This decision to reject Jesus is actually refusing the gift of reconciliation—the heart of salvation.

WE NEED THIS GIFT

Why do we need to accept this gift of salvation? We have all fallen short of who God intended us to be. The only way to reconnect with God is to acknowledge this truth and choose to receive His free gift. The Bible says:

✠ *...for all have sinned and fall short of the glory of God* (Romans 3:23).

The word for sin in Hebrew is *hamartia* (ham-ar-tee-ah) which means "missing the mark" or "taking the wrong course." The New Testament uses the word in a number of ways: in a generic sense for a concrete wrongdoing; as a principle and quality of action; and as a sinful deed.[1] The word for sin was also used as an archers' term for an arrow that misses its mark or target.

Can we hit that target on our own? See if you qualify according to this entry requirement:

✠ [Jesus said] *"Be perfect, therefore, as your heavenly Father is perfect"* (Matthew 5:48).

Working our way to Heaven by being good or following rules is simply *not* an option. This is why the gift of life is a *gift*, because we alone are not able to earn it even if we desired to. The Old Testament chronicles a very long history where men and women did their very best to earn their salvation. Even then, God required animal sacrifices to atone, or pay, for sin, creating an endless cycle—forever missing the mark. But when He sent His Son, the story changed.

✠ *For this reason He* [Jesus] *had to be made like his brothers* [you and me] *in every way, in order that He might become a merciful and faithful high priest in service to God, and that He might make* **atonement** *for the sins of the people* (Hebrews 2:17).

The English word *atone* is formed by joining two words together, *at* and *one*. It means to become *at one* with God or reconciled with Him. This is the state which God wishes to see our spirit and His Spirit–in oneness. In this verse Jesus is clearly the way for us to achieve this oneness of spirits. No other way is possible.

So while we see it was by the sin of one (Adam) that death was passed to all, it is by the death of One (Jesus) that life is passed to all who accept it. Now, those born once physically, die twice (physically and spiritually), but those born twice, die only once (physically).

Maybe you're a really good person. You do good things. You don't have any obvious sins in your life. Who knows, perhaps you even go to church every week. However, in God's eyes you have fallen short even if you've only sinned once. Even *one* sin makes you incapable of being holy, pure, and blameless:

☩ *For whoever keeps the whole law and yet stumbles at just* **one** *point is guilty of breaking* **all** *of it* (James 2:10).

Let's look at it this way: if you had a reservoir of clean water and you poured even the smallest amount of poison in it, the whole reservoir would be poisoned. No one could drink from it; and since God is perfectly pure, He can't drink from it either. Remember that there is *no* darkness found in Him. Many mistakenly believe that they need to change their lives, quit sinning, and become perfect to receive the gift of salvation. However, the reservoir will always be poisoned and toxic—Jesus Christ, the gift through which salvation is received, is the only renewing Source to purify our reservoir.

Remember Jesus asking the Samaritan woman at the well for a drink? He was thirsty for fellowship with her, but her well was not living water. Jesus needs to purify our wells into living water so they together can quench that thirst for fellowship.

✠ *As for you, you were dead in your transgressions and sins, in which you used to live when you followed the ways of this world and of the ruler of the kingdom of the air, the spirit who is now at work in those who are disobedient. All of us also lived among them at one time, gratifying the cravings of our sinful nature and following its desires and thoughts. Like the rest, we were by nature objects of wrath. But because of His great love for us, God, Who is rich in mercy, made us alive with Christ even when we were dead in transgressions—it is by grace you have been saved. And God raised us up with Christ and seated us with Him in heavenly realms in Christ Jesus in order that in the coming age He might show the incomparable riches of His grace, expressed in his kindness to us in Christ Jesus. For it is by* **grace** *you have been saved, through faith—and this not from yourselves, it is the* **gift** *of God—not by works, so that no man can boast* (Ephesians 2:1-9).

The gift of salvation which Jesus embodies is a *gift*, pure and simple. We can't earn or attain this salvation on our own. We receive this gift by the *grace* of God. The concept of grace is unique to the Christian faith. Other religions teach the idea of Karma which is the philosophy according to which the quality of people's current and future lives is determined only by *their* behavior in this life. Jesus offers us *grace*—which can be defined as unmerited or undeserved favor. The word for grace, *charis*, comes from the same root as chara, which means "joy" or chairo "to rejoice."[2] What a perfect origin for such a word! Grace brings people real joy because it offers freedom—freedom from past mistakes, to walk in the truth that God accepts and loves you unconditionally, no matter what you've done in the past—*no matter what you have done in the past.* Jesus Christ's sacrifice cleans the reservoir so you can reconnect with God. If it were up to you to do good works—to earn your salvation, you would become *enslaved* to your efforts. How many good deeds would you need to perform? How would you ever know if you'd done enough?

God's plan is simple: accept His gift and by His grace you are set free! There is only one way to receive eternal life and freedom, we have to *believe* Jesus was sacrificed to make atonement for our sins.

⊕ *God presented Him [Jesus] as a sacrifice of atonement, through faith in His blood. He did this to demonstrate His justice, because in for-bearance He had left the sins committed beforehand unpunished—* [by those in the Old Testament who had faith in the prophesied Messiah to come] (Romans 3:25).

Also in the New Testament Book of Romans there is an explanation about how to ask for and receive this gift:

⊕ *If you **confess** with your mouth, "Jesus is Lord," and **believe** in your heart that God raised him from the dead, you will be **saved**. For it is with your heart that you believe and are justified, and it is with your mouth that you confess and are saved* (Romans 10:9-10).

Let me talk for a moment about the word *believe.* We use it rather care-lessly in the world today. We talk about believing in a cause or Peter Pan or as a hesitant response to someone's question, "I believe so." *Believe* in Romans 10:9-10 is the word *pisteuo* (pist-yoo-oh), the verb form of *pistis*, which means "faith" or "to be fully convinced of" or "to rely on."[3] We are not simply talking about having a belief that Jesus existed. Many people believe He existed, perhaps seeing Him as a prophet or great spiritual leader; however, they *don't* believe in Him for their salvation. Even demons believe Jesus was the Son of God:

✝ *"What do you want with us, Son of God?" they* [the demons] *shouted. "Have you come here to torture us before the appointed time?"* (Matthew 8:29)

Perhaps you know people who pray to Jesus in times of trouble, but don't believe in Him for salvation. This is called temporal faith. People with temporal faith believe in Jesus only for temporal things, such as a winning team, a new car, house, job, fame, health, money, things that are not eternal. This kind of faith or belief in Jesus does *not* give them eternal salvation.

It is important to truly believe and trust in the right source for your eternal salvation. There is a story of a high-wire tight rope artist who asked a man in the crowd if he believed he could cross over the high wire stretched across a deep canyon. The man looked at the situation and nonchalantly said "yes." So the high-wire artist asked him to get into a wheelbarrow and he would take him across. What the man *believed* took on a whole new meaning when the stakes were raised and his life *depended* on what he *believed.*

You are going to die at some point. When this happens we all hope to cross over that canyon of death into a new and better life of some kind after we die. Who are you trusting to get you across that high wire? It's an *important* question. The *most* important question you will ever have to answer in this life. Both failing to properly answer and procrastinating lead to the same disastrous result—trusting in *yourself.* Are you *really* qualified to be your own master of eternal life and death?

The Bible clearly says the eternal gift of salvation only comes through *believing in Jesus as your Savior.* Nothing more, and nothing less.

✠ [Jesus said] *"I tell you the truth, whoever hears My words and believes Him who sent Me has eternal life and will not be condemned; he has **crossed** over from death to **life**"* (John 5:24).

ACTION & VISUALIZATION

Accept God's gift of salvation—picture yourself drinking living water.

AN EASY GIFT TO RECEIVE

I am belaboring this point because it is important for you to completely understand: there is no way to earn or work your way into salvation, it is an unmerited free *gift*—a gift of grace. Read what happened to a criminal who hung next to Jesus at His crucifixion:

✠ *One of the criminals who hung there hurled insults at Him: "Aren't You the Christ? Save Yourself and us!" But the other criminal rebuked him. "Don't you fear God," he said, "since you are under the same sentence? We are punished justly, for we are getting what our deeds deserve. But this Man has done nothing wrong." Then he said, "Jesus, remember me when You come into Your Kingdom." Jesus answered him, "I tell you the truth, today you will be with Me in paradise"* (Luke 23:39-43).

The sinner on the cross only had to believe in who Jesus was—the Savior—to receive the gift of salvation. Jesus said his confession of faith would save him, "Today you will be with Me in paradise." The criminal didn't have the time or ability to come down from his cross and be a good person, or perform some kind of repentant act. He only had to believe in his heart and confess with his mouth that Jesus is the Savior.

Jesus wants you to come to Him the same way—just as you are. His entire ministry revolved around reaching out to the most hardened sinners, the broken, downtrodden people of the day. Interestingly, Jesus was criticized by the religious leaders of the time for hanging out with sinful, immoral people. In fact, Jesus wanted the people around Him (and us as well) to understand He came to forgive the sins of *all* sinners. He told this insightful story, as recorded in the Gospel of Luke:

Now one of the Pharisees invited Jesus to have dinner with Him, so He went to the Pharisee's house and reclined at the table. When a woman who had lived a sinful life in that town learned that Jesus was eating at the Pharisee's house, she brought an alabaster jar of perfume, and as she stood behind Him at His feet weeping, she began to wet His feet with her tears. Then she wiped them with her hair, kissed them and poured perfume on them. When the Pharisee who had invited Him saw this, he said to himself, "If this Man were a prophet, He would know who is touching Him and what kind of woman she is—that she is a sinner." Jesus answered him, "Simon, I have something to tell you." "Tell me, Teacher," he said. [Jesus answered] "Two men owed money to a certain moneylender. One owed him five hundred denarii, and the other fifty. Neither of them had the money to pay him back, so he canceled the debts of both. Now which of them will love him more?" Simon replied, "I suppose the one who had the bigger debt canceled." "You have judged correctly," Jesus said. Then he turned toward the woman and said to Simon, "Do you see this woman? I came into your [the pharisee's] house. You did not give Me any water for My feet, but she wet My feet with her tears and wiped them with her hair. You did not give Me a kiss, but this woman, from the time I entered, has not stopped kissing My feet. You did not put oil on My head, but she has poured perfume on My feet. Therefore, I tell you, her many sins have been forgiven—for she loved much. But he who has been forgiven little loves little."...Jesus said to the woman, "Your faith has saved you; go in peace" (Luke 7:36-47,50).

Jesus told the woman her faith had saved her. The word for "save" in the original text, *sozo* (sode-zoe), means "to rescue from danger or destruction" or "to deliver." Perhaps you've heard someone ask the question, "Are you saved?" They are asking if *the person has accepted God's gift of salvation."*[4] It's a fair and important question. But it would be wrong to assume a "yes" answer, and to end the discussion there.

To be saved is just the starting point for a renewed relationship with God; His saving power touches every area of your life. He doesn't just want you to reconnect with Him—he wants you to get to *know* Him, to *learn* to *live life as He intended.* He wants you to *engage* Him in your life and to receive all the gifts He offers that lead to an intimate relationship. The role of free choice continues even after we accept God's *first* Gift.

How does this relationship grow? The apostle Paul alluded to this in his letter to the church at Philippi:

*Therefore, my dear friends, as you have always obeyed—not only in my presence, but now much more in my absence—**continue to work out your salvation** with fear and trembling* (Philippians 2:12).

After you accept your gift of salvation, you start a journey, learning how to walk in relationship with God. A relationship that will cause you to change some of your thinking and ways of acting if you are going to receive the full benefit of this gift and other gifts while you are still on earth.

Read what Jesus prayed right before His death:

My prayer is not for them alone. I pray also for those who will believe in Me through their message, that all of them may be one, Father, just as You are in Me and I am in You. May they also be in Us so that the world may believe that You have sent Me. I have given them the glory that You gave Me, that they may be one as We are One: I in them and You in Me. May they be brought to complete unity [with God and His will for your life] *to let the world know that You sent Me and have loved **them** even as You have loved **Me*** (John 17:20-23).

Jesus wants to start giving back the glory God intended for you—a flicker at first, and a full blaze in the life to come.

Perhaps you haven't yet accepted Christ as your Savior. You may be wondering, "How do I know that what these verses are saying is true?" That's where faith enters the picture. Read this passage written by the apostle John:

*Anyone who believes in the Son of God **has this testimony in his heart**. Anyone who does not believe God has made Him out to be a liar, because he has not believed the testimony God has given about His Son. And this is the testimony: God has given us eternal life, and this life is in His Son. He who has the Son has life; he who does not have the Son of God does not have life* (1 John 5:10-12).

When your spirit comes alive, you will *know* all this to be true in your heart. Once you begin a relationship with Jesus, your spirit and God's in you will be as real to you as this book you're holding. Until then, the verses may seem empty—just words on a page.

Some well-intentioned Christians only throw Bible verses at people to get them to accept Jesus. God's Word certainly is a powerful thing. But for some, hearing God's Word alone does little to bring them to Him if they're not open to it. He wants *willing* companions. Even God's Word cannot save you; it is by your faith in Christ alone.

When I walked into a church in 1988, I had plenty of unresolved issues in my life and just as many questions on my mind. No one stood next to me and quoted Bible verses to bring me to Christ. I was seeking God, so God reached out in a very real, experiential way. After I accepted Jesus as my Savior, I knew immediately there was something very different in me. There was something new in me, a change from the *inside out* that allowed me to make sense of things. God's method is to work from the *inside out*, giving you a completely new perspective.

I wanted to tell the world about my new perspective. But how? It was as if I had received sight for the first time in a world filled with blindness. How could I possibly explain that experience to someone who was still blind—who had always known blindness? What would I tell them about the color blue? About the infinite variations of a smile? About the uniqueness of every sunset?

This also works in reverse. Consider the book you're holding. You are aware of its reality, and there is nothing anybody can say that will convince you it isn't real. You know you are holding this book because…you're holding it! Nobody is going to come up with a reasonable argument that will cause you to believe otherwise. This is how being born again works, too. You know God is in you because…God is in you! Until you experience it yourself, you can't know what it's like. Someone could describe it to you until they're blue in the face, but without the actual experience, it's simply impossible to *fully* understand.

ACTION & VISUALIZATION
Reach out to God and trust Him to show you the way.

GOD SPEAKS THROUGH HIS CREATION

God knows it can be difficult to accept the truth of His story. While it ultimately takes faith to believe, God has generously given us clues in nature that point to Him:

✝ *God has made it plain to them* [humankind]. *For since the creation of the world God's invisible qualities—His eternal power and divine nature—have been clearly seen, being understood from what has been made, so that men are without excuse* [to know He exists and created everything] (Romans 1:19-20).

You only have to look at the complexity of this world to know it was planned and created by an Intelligent Designer. If you were walking along the beach and saw a complex arrangement of sand that spelled out "Jane loves Bill" you would probably assume it was written by an *intelligent being* and *not* the random rearrangement of sand caused by waves.

Using the same perspective, let's look at the complexity of life itself, substantially more complex than just words written in the sand. Protein chains made up in links called amino acids are the most basic ingredients to create life. These amino acids have to line up in exactly the right order and *all* be left handed (which is in itself against the tendency of nature to naturally occur). A small protein with only 100 amino acids would only have 1 chance of occurring in 10,000,000,000,000,000,000,000,000, 000,000,000,000,000,000,000,000,000,000,000,000,000,000,000,000,00 0,000,000,000,000,000,000,000,000,000,000,000,000,000,000,000 (10 to the 129th power). Proteins with 400 amino acids would have considerably worse odds than this.[5] Moreover, you need *many, many different* kinds of proteins to begin to create life and these odds have to be replicated *many, many times* over before resulting in the *simplest* of living organisms. That statistical number would fill this page! If you're betting on luck or some kind of natural process to create life, stay away from Las Vegas!

Indeed if you took these statistical numbers to a mathematician they would tell you anything that has over 10 to the 50th power of happening is statistically impossible. Yet evolutionists rely on one statistically impossible event after another to supposedly give us a "scientific" view about the origination of life. Sadly many people today are betting their eternal life on these impossible odds. It is obvious an Intelligent Designer arranges all the details in such a way as to allow living things to function in extremely complex and interdependent ways.

Professor Chandra Wickramasinghe and Sir Fred Hoyle—whose ten-year study calculated the statistical odds of our life coming about by chance to 1 in 10 to the 40,000th power—summed it up rather imaginatively with this statistical calculation: the likelihood of a "lucky" circumstance creating life was about the equivalent to the probability of a tornado sweeping through a junkyard and assembling a fully functional Boeing 747 actually in flight out the other side.[6] In fact, it's interesting to note there are approximately 4.5 million non-flying parts (parts that could not fly alone without being organized in just a certain way with the other parts) in the plane; however, in just *one* human cell there are over *one billion* non-living parts which *must* be organized in just a certain way for that one cell to function. You would never trust your life on a plane where you didn't know its parts had been organized by an intelligent designer. So why would you put your trust in a theory that has *never* been proven and indeed according to mathematicians is statistically impossible to happen?

Moreover, the creation of life itself through evolution would defy the laws of nature as we know them. The Second Law of Thermodynamics (a law fully accepted by all) states in simple terms the natural tendency is for information to get scrambled—order tends to move into disorder (things are wearing out or breaking down) not organizing into higher more complicated forms. This is important and one of the most provable laws of physics. This means our universe, left to its own natural process, tends toward maximum entropy (a measure of disorder).[7] An example would be if you parked a '57 Chevy on the beach. Eventually it would become a pile of rusted-out junk. But if you took a pile of rusted-out junk onto the beach, you would never end up with a drivable '57 Chevy. Loss of *organization* is the natural progression of nature. Organization requires an *organizer*.

God created the earth with precision, and the Bible says that God is focused on every detail of *you*.

✠ *And even the very hairs of your head are all numbered* [by God] (Matthew 10:30).

Let's go even deeper and consider just a *few* of the many, many, many amazing details about how you were designed and how the world was created for your benefit. Consider:

In the typical human baby, God *organizes* approximately 3,000,000,000,000,000,000,000,000,000 atoms in such a way as to create a living creature that will not remain the same, but will grow or *organize* itself over time in generally the same form, but with some exceptions. To accomplish this growth or *organization* He has imbedded in each of us a DNA map that guides growth or *organization* from baby to adult, each according to our own unique plan.

Does this seem like an accident of nature to you? Evolutionists have *not* come up with any credible theory to explain how or where these plans of construction embedded in our DNA come from. DNA instructs all parts of the body to capture the materials it needs and then it *mysteriously* orders the constitution of them in a certain order to make life and grow all living things. I say mysteriously because there is one unexplained fact after another in the formation and sustaining of life. Truth is, we can't even fully explain today how He did it, but we do know God used the DNA mapping plan for the *organization* and construction of plants, animals, fish, birds, insects, every living thing. In each cell of any seed or living being you can find the entire growth or *organizing* plan for that specific living thing; a plan that governs how it *organizes* the many new atoms required in its growth.

During the human baby's growth to an adult it will assimilate in an *organized* fashion according to its DNA plan an additional 67,000,000,000,000,000,000,000,000,000 atoms. Just having the material isn't enough to grow a baby. It's the information and mechanism for arranging that material that is important. Imagine you forgot someone's phone number that had these same 29 digits. How long would it take you to randomly find the right order of numbers? The answer is not in your lifetime or even the earth's age according to evolutionists.

On a different level, the immune system with incredible sophistication and complexity, was designed and *organized* by God to fight germs, viruses, and other micro organisms. The human brain is a natural computer composed of 100 billion neurons, each of which connects to about 10,000 others, and *all* of which function in parallel. Your brain is processing an uncountable amount of information every second. The eye *alone* collects enough data for the brain in just 1/10 of a second to keep a Cray supercomputer processing for 100 years.[8]

The body is designed and *organized* to assimilate the daily required fuel, vitamins, minerals, and nutrients needed to sustain itself. Each one of the processes is unbelievably complex and involved. For example, the body must maintain its internal temperature within a tenth of a degree range or vitamin B won't be assimilated.

All these things, and many more necessities for sustenance, are supplied by an extremely complicated, delicate, and interdependent supply chain within the world we live. Many small differences (changes to temperature, the Earth's orbit, etc.) would immobilize the structure that supplies our needs and would cause humans to become extinct.

Amazingly, the average human heart will beat, in an average lifetime, 2.7 billion times consecutively without interruption or time off.

Given the unbelievable complexity and organization to create and sustain life, it certainly seems unlikely that a statistically *impossible* series of random events created and sustains your life, don't you think?

Perhaps more importantly, how would a soul come about by a random process? Or our self-awareness? Our intellect? Emotions? Desires? Our ability to love? Could *all* of this come from a series of *accidents*?

THE RELATIONSHIP BETWEEN BODY, MIND AND SPIRIT

God put an incredible amount of thought and purpose into the inner working of our physical bodies. He put equal thought and purpose into the creation of our minds (our intellect and emotions)—with which we make our decisions using our free will—and spirits, which can act like navigation systems when they're connected with the Creator. Just as your body is charged with gathering physical information to help you navigate through life, your spirit is charged with gathering spiritual information.

Your mind is constantly *balancing* between the *body* and *spirit* on this journey through life. Imagine an airplane cockpit with only half of its vital instruments working. What if the missing equipment included the communications system (there goes your dialogue with the control tower) and the navigational system (there goes your ability to choose a destination and the directions to get there)? This lack of critical equipment is similar to our condition before we are born again—before we're reconnected with God.

There is a complex interdependent relationship between the physical life (body and mind) and the spiritual life. This becomes especially evident when we begin to consider difficult issues such as sin, immorality, and what happens when we die. Too often, we focus on the physical aspects of this life without regard for the spiritual. The spiritual truths that affect our life everyday. Our constant focus on pursuing and gratifying our bodies' needs can distract us from discovering spiritual realities. However, *if we're open to God*, He can even use this pursuit of the physical to point us to spiritual truth. One great example of this is found in the story of Bartimaeus:

Then they came to Jericho. As Jesus and His disciples, together with a large crowd, were leaving the city, a blind man, Bartimaeus (that is, the Son of Timaeus), was sitting by the roadside begging. When he heard that it was Jesus of Nazareth, he began to shout, "Jesus, Son of David, have mercy on me!" Many rebuked him and told him to be quiet, but he shouted all the more, "Son of David, have mercy on me!" Jesus stopped and said, "Call him." So they called to the blind man, "Cheer up! On your feet! He's calling you." Throwing his cloak aside, he jumped to his feet and came to Jesus. "What do you want Me to do for you?" Jesus asked him (Mark 10:46-51).

At this point in the story you may be wondering, "Why on earth would Jesus ask him such a question?" It would seem obvious that a blind man would want to see, right? Jesus is aware of another reality, a spiritual reality. Bartimaeus had a bigger problem than his *physical* blindness—he was *spiritually* blind. While his physical blindness would only last during his living years, spiritual blindness *affected his eternity*. Jesus knew the blind man's *biggest* need was for eternal salvation—to recognize Jesus as the Messiah and choose to follow Him. Bartimaeus did this when he acknowledged Jesus as "Son of David."

The Jews were expecting a Messiah—a Savior who would bring salvation to their nation. The Old Testament taught that the Messiah would come from the lineage of King David. Jesus was indeed from King David's lineage. He was also the prophesied Messiah, though many Jews did not choose to believe it. However, Bartimaeus, because of his statement, *did* show belief in Jesus as the Messiah—and because of that, he was given the gift of salvation in addition to his sight that day.

YOUR STORY SO FAR

Where are you? God asked Adam and Eve this question and He asks you now: "Where are you spiritually?" Have you already chosen to accept God's first gift—the gift of salvation? Or are you still on your spiritual quest? If you're still searching, perhaps it's because you're still unsure how Jesus really fits into your story. Perhaps you believe He was just a prophet, or a teacher, or some sort of philosopher. Read what the Bible says about who Jesus is:

*He is the image of the invisible God, the Firstborn over all creation. For by Him **all** things were created: things in Heaven and on earth, visible and invisible, whether thrones or powers or rulers or authorities; all things were created by Him and for Him. He is before all things, and in Him all things hold together. And He is the **head** of the body, the Church; He is the beginning and the Firstborn from among the dead, so that in **everything** He might have the **supremacy**. For God was pleased to have all **His fullness dwell in Him**, and through Him to **reconcile** to Himself all things, whether things on earth or things in Heaven, by making peace through His blood, shed on the Cross. Once you were alienated from God and were enemies in your minds because of your evil behavior. But now He has **reconciled** you by **Christ's physical body through death** to present you holy in His sight* [Christ's blood covers your sins], *without blemish and free from accusation...* (Colossians 1:15-22).

Jesus is *the* key to our reconciliation with God. Accepting the gift of salvation is as simple as doing what Bartimaeus did or what the criminal next to Jesus on the Cross did. They *recognized* and *trusted* Him as their *Savior.* So what about you? Where are you? You may not be blind like Bartimaeus or hanging on a cross like the thief, but do you feel as helpless as they did? "Jesus have mercy on me." "Jesus remember me." Have you trusted in Jesus as the *only One* who can save you? This is the first gift that *must be accepted and used* for it to have any *value.* This is what brings us back on course. Jesus Christ is *the* way to *life.* Perhaps *now* is the time for you to make that decision.

If you're ready for this gift and wish to begin a relationship with God, all you have to do is believe in your heart and respond in prayer, much like the following:

✝ *Jesus, I confess that I'm a sinner and I come to You through my faith. I invite You into my heart and into my life right now. I confess with my mouth that You are Lord of my life. I believe You died for my sins and that God raised You from the dead so that I might have everlasting life with You. Thank You for taking my place on the Cross and for paying the full price for my sins. Fill me with Your Holy Spirit and make my life pleasing and fruitful in Your sight. I am praying in the name of Jesus. Amen.*

If you just took that first step, congratulations! It is your Birthday, the first day of your new life connected to God. The Bible tells us in Luke 15:22-24 that whenever someone accepts the gift of salvation, a celebration breaks out in Heaven. God throws a party just for you. We find the beautiful picture of this celebration in the story of the Prodigal Son which Jesus relays to us in Luke. This is the story of a man and his two sons. One son leaves home abruptly, taking all of his inheritance with him and abandoning his family to live life on his own—the way he wants to. Eventually, he ends up broke, empty, and alone. Out of sheer desperation he returns home, expecting very little from his father because of all the wrongs he has done. Jesus continues the rest of the story:

✠ [The prodigal son says] *"I will set out and go back to my father and say to him: Father, I have sinned against Heaven and against you. I am no longer worthy to be called your son; make me like one of your hired men." So he got up and went to his father. But while he was still a long way off, his father saw him and was **filled with compassion for him**; he ran to his son, threw his arms around him and kissed him* (Luke 15:18-20).

Did you notice what it says about the father? He saw his son while he was *a long way off*. The father was looking for him, *expecting* him, ready to accept him. What a beautiful picture. Your heavenly Father has been compassionately expecting you, too. Jesus continues the story:

✠ *The son said to him, "Father, I have **sinned** against Heaven and against you. I am no longer worthy to be called your son." But the father said to his servants, "Quick! Bring the best robe and put it on him. Put a ring on his finger and sandals on his feet. Bring the fattened calf and kill it. Let's have a **feast** and **celebrate**. For this son of mine was dead and is **alive again**; he was lost and is found." So they began to celebrate* (Luke 15:21-24).

While this is a marvelous story of reconciliation, it also shows God accepts, even welcomes, those of us who accept the gift of salvation, in spite of our sin against Him, our heavenly Father. Those of us who were spiritually dead are alive—we're "born again." Jesus continues:

✠ *Meanwhile, the older son was in the field. When he came near the house, he heard music and dancing. So he called one of the servants and asked him what was going on. "Your brother has come," he replied, "and your father has killed the fattened calf because he has him back safe and sound." The older brother became angry and refused to go in. So his father went out and pleaded with him. But he answered his father, "Look! All these years I've been slaving for you and never disobeyed your orders. Yet you never gave me even a young goat so I could celebrate with my friends. But when this son of yours who has squandered your property with prostitutes comes home, you kill the fattened calf for him!"* (Luke 15:25-30)

Some people may have a hard time accepting the fact that God has *accepted you*. They might look at the way you've lived—the actions that preceded your acceptance of this first gift—and question your salvation or your right to it. Here's a truth that's important to understand: your salvation is between *you* and *God*. It doesn't matter what other people believe—if you've been saved, you've been saved. Don't be discouraged or offended by what others may say. Some people may even be jealous of your new life. But read what Jesus said the father says to the son who had not run away:

*"My son," the father said, "you are always with me, and everything I have is yours. But we had to celebrate and be glad, because this brother of yours was **dead** and is **alive again**; he was lost and is found"* (Luke 15:31-32).

SATAN'S PLAN

Yes, God is celebrating, but, as you might guess, there is another who gets angry when someone accepts the gift of salvation. Reconnecting to the Source of light allows people to bring God's light into the world at an ever-increasing level. Satan's goal is to stop or limit your light from shining in the world because light limits him in the world. The parable of the sower reveals this reality:

✠ [Jesus said] *"As he was scattering the seed, some fell along the path, and the birds came and ate it up. Some fell on rocky places, where it did not have much soil. It sprang up quickly, because the soil was shallow. But when the sun came up, the plants were scorched, and they withered because they had no root. Other seed fell among thorns, which grew up and choked the plants, so that they did not bear grain. Still other seed fell on good soil. It came up, grew and produced a crop, multiplying thirty, sixty, or even a hundred times"* (Mark 4:4-8).

When asked to explain the parable Jesus said:

✠ *The farmer sows the word* [of God]. *Some people are like seed along the path, where the word is sown. As soon as they hear it, satan comes and takes away the word that was sown in them. Others, like seed sown on rocky places, hear the word and at once receive it with joy. But since they have no root, they last only a short time. When trouble or persecution comes because of the word, they quickly fall away. Still others, like seed sown among thorns, hear the word; but the worries of this life, the deceitfulness of wealth and the desires for other things come in and choke the word, making it unfruitful. Others, like seed sown on good soil, hear the word, accept it, and produce a crop—thirty, sixty or even a hundred times what was sown"* (Mark 4:14-20).

This parable explains how people respond when presented with the gift of salvation. And it's clear from Jesus' explanation that satan would love to "take away the Word that was sown" in you. He despises those who follow God and he will do anything to keep you from reflecting the image and likeness of God into the world.

One of satan's greatest tactics is to sow uncertainty in your heart. Perhaps you begin to wonder, "Am I really accepted by God?" Surely you've failed too many times. Right?

Wrong. That's satan talking. Don't listen to him:

✟ [Jesus said] *"He* [the devil] *was a murderer from the beginning, not holding to the truth, for there is no truth in him. When he lies, he speaks his native language, for he is a liar and the father of lies* (John 8:44).

The truth is:

✟ *If we confess our sins, He is faithful and just and will forgive us our sins and purify us from all unrighteousness* (1 John 1:9).

Uncertainty and doubt aren't the only methods satan uses to keep that seed from growing all-important roots in your heart. He sends tribulation and persecution to make you stumble. I believe that choosing to follow God by accepting this gift doesn't magically make life perfect. We still live in an imperfect fallen world and life will be full of trials and challenges as you deal with it. You will still face temptation. Salvation does not make you immune to greed, sexual immorality, pride, addiction—the desire to satisfy the flesh. However, God gives you the power through the Holy Spirit to resist temptations and to weather the storms of life.

You will come to realize that physical cravings don't satisfy. Just like the prodigal son, the thief on the cross, the blind man, and you and I—we know the Way, the Truth and Life; all these worldly desires pale in comparison.

If you've accepted God's gift of salvation, you are the "good ground" Jesus referred to in the parable—you have become imperishable and eternal. The only question that remains is how much *you* will *choose* to grow in this life:

✟ *For you have been born again, not of perishable seed, but of imperishable...*(1 Peter 1:23).

How much you grow depends on how much you cultivate the seed planted in you by God, and follow the instructions you are given:

✟ [Jesus said] *"But the seed on good soil stands for those with a noble and good heart, who hear the word, retain it, and by **persevering** produce a crop"* (Luke 8:15).

As we go through the Bible together, you will grow spiritually and your light will shine more brightly through perseverance.

MEDITATION POINT

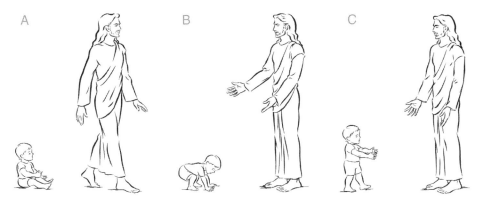

Trials, errors and determination will allow you to walk like Him. You must first make the attempt though to actually even do it.

Go to Chapter 2 in the Study Guide section on page 275.

ENDNOTES

1. Jack Hayford, ed., *Spirit-Filled Life Bible for Students* (Nashville, TN: Thomas Nelson, 1995), 1339.

2. Ibid., 1510.

3. Ibid., 1453.

4. Ibid., 1297-1298.

5. Duane T. Gish, *The Amazing Story of Creation: From Science and the Bible* (Green Forest, AR: Master Books, 1996).

6. Ibid., 34-35.

7. Paul S. Taylor, *The Illustrated Origins Answer Book, Fifth Edition* (Gilbert, AZ: Eden Communications, 1995), 7-8.

8. Michael Denton, *Evolution: A Theory in Crisis* (Chevy Chase, MD: Adler & Adler Publishers, Inc., 1986), 310.

Chapter 3

GIFT #1—LIFE (PART 2)

HOW DO YOU GET THE MOST FROM IT?

Before you begin to read, pray that the Holy Spirit
will give you understanding and application.

✝ *Do you not know that in a race all the runners run, but only one gets
the prize? Run in such a way as to get the prize. Everyone who com-
petes in the games goes into strict training. They do it to get a crown
that will not last; but we do it to get a crown that will last forever.
Therefore I do not run like a man running aimlessly; I do not fight
like a man beating the air. No, I beat my body and make it my slave
so that after I have preached to others, I myself will not be disquali-
fied for the prize* (1 Corinthians 9:24-27).

"OK, I'VE OPENED THIS GIFT OF LIFE. NOW WHAT?"

As a child, when you got that brand-new bike for Christmas, did you
quickly put it in a storage closet? Or how about now if you received
a new 50-inch plasma television or state-of-the-art laptop computer—would you leave them in the boxes? Would you toss a velvet jewelry

box in a drawer, unopened? Of course not! These new gifts cry out to be opened, examined, and used.

If it was snowing outside on Christmas Day, you probably rode your new bike around the living room. After tearing open the boxes, I remember calling friends in excitement about my new gifts—it's was a joyful and exciting occasion. I could hardly wait to unwrap and use these new gifts.

So what about this wonderful *gift of life*? Well, *unlike* toys and clothing we eventually grow out or tired of, the gift of life will make our lives exciting to live—every day here on earth and especially after we die. The gift of life that God offers enriches our daily lives—gives us purpose and meaning. The gift of life assures us that we will spend eternity in the presence of a God who loves us unconditionally, who has only our very best interests at the top of His priority list. Unwrapping and using this gift will bring joy and confidence to your life. God gives you this gift so if you choose daily to use it you can have an abundantly joyful life now, and an eternal life of blessings with Him.

✠ [Jesus said] *"...I have come that they may have **life** and that they may have it more **abundantly*** (John 10:10 NKJV).

✠ [Jesus said to his disciples before He was crucified] *"In my Father's house are many rooms; if it were not so, I would have told you* [and us]. *I am going there to prepare a place for you, I will come back and take you to be with Me that you will also may be where I am"* (John 14:2-3).

When we're born again, we're in many ways like newborn babies. We need to grow up, to mature into adulthood. In our case, that means growing into the image and likeness of God. This is a *daily* choice—something we are encouraged, even commanded to pursue. This kind of growth doesn't just happen magically, it requires *your active involvement.*

✠ *For we are God's workmanship, created in Christ Jesus to do good works, which God prepared in advance for us to do* (Ephesians 2:10).

What are you pursuing? What is most important to you? We can't pursue everything all the time and be successful and fulfilled. We have to make choices with our time and efforts to be successful in our pursuits. What do you pursue?

The desire for happiness is always near the top of the list in any survey exploring what people want out of life. We put great effort into what we think will make us happy, spending the majority of our time earning money to buy things to bring us closer to this elusive feeling of happiness. This is one of life's core desires. But here's the problem: we were not created to be fulfilled from the *outside in.* God originally designed us to achieve our fulfillment from the *inside out.* God has "hardwired" His creation for something far greater than happiness—He designed us for *joy* and *blessings;* these have eternal qualities.

As you grow in faith—the substance of your life—finding fulfillment will shift from the pursuit of outer activities to an inner fulfillment. This comes through a new life in God, a relationship which is initially internally developed. Beyond happiness, a dynamic and growing relationship with Christ will allow you to cultivate joy from within and receive blessings from your Creator as He intended for you.

Consider the word *happy.* It has the same root as the word *happenstance* or *happening.* With this meaning in mind, we could assume that to be happy we must *make fun things happen* continually—forever chasing that goal. However, this obsession with "making fun things happen" turns us into mice running on wheels trying to keep the good times rolling.

Eventually, bad things will *always* happen and therefore the pursuit of happiness is ultimately destined to *fail*. However, regardless of how many times we try and fail, we are relentless. We're running, we're working, we're always busy, but we can't seem to get any closer to our goal of real sustained happiness because "being happy" is a momentary or temporal state. It doesn't last.

The real question is, *"How do we find joy?"*

As Christ *grows* within you, you'll discover that *joy* and *blessings* surpass happiness because they come from within. Read what the Bible says about this:

✠ *...strength and joy* [are] *in His* [God's] *dwelling place* (1 Chronicles 16:27).

✠ *Do not grieve, for the joy of the Lord is your strength* (Nehemiah 8:10).

✠ *You have filled my heart with greater joy than when their grain and new wine abound* (Psalm 4:7).

✠ *You* [God] *have made known to me the path of life; You will fill me with joy in your presence...*(Psalm 16:11).

✠ [Jesus said] *"I have told you this* [the instructions in the Bible] *so that My joy may be in you and that your joy may be complete"* (John 15:11).

✠ *Blessed is he who comes in the name of the Lord... (Psalm 118:26).*

✠ *But the man who looks intently into the perfect law [the Bible] that gives freedom, and continues to do this, not forgetting what he has heard, but doing it—he will be blessed in what he does (James 1:25).*

✠ [God said] *"If you follow My decrees and are careful to obey My commands, I will send you rain in its season, and the ground will yield its crops and the trees of the field their fruit. Your threshing will continue until the grape harvest and the grape harvest will continue until planting, and you will eat all the food you want and live safely in your land. I will grant peace in the land, and you will lie down and no one will make you afraid. I will remove the savage beasts and the sword will not pass through your country"* (Leviticus 26:3-6).

There are physical and spiritual blessings. It is also important to note in the last verse in the Leviticus passage that blessings come "in season"—that's a season that God determines, not us. Physically we may have bad times, but our God-given joy and blessings will get us through the bad circumstances as well as the good because they come from within and are not reliant on outside circumstances. Happiness is temporary, bound by circumstances and feelings. Blessings and joy are infinite, without change, when we access them from within. The root word for *blessing, makar,* means "the same" or "permanent." This is the very nature of God—eternal.

As I've mentioned before, you will not be immune to bad circumstances after you become a Christian; however, when they do happen you can have an *inner* peace, strength, and joy. This probably sounds unbelievable to you now, but just like the experience of coming to know Christ, once you've experienced it—you'll know exactly what I'm talking about. Joy is deep within and does not depend on external circumstance—it comes when you are living *in* His image and likeness, *in* close relationship with Him.

RUNNING THE RACE

This chapter began with a verse where the apostle Paul compares our life here on earth to running a race. Preparing for a race is a lot like the way we're to approach our spiritual development. It is something we have to *pursue*—something we have to work at with *purpose*. If you set out to run a marathon, you would have to change your habits so your body and mind are in peak condition. Your lifestyle would have to change for you to be successful. The same principle holds true for developing spiritually.

Paul reminds us that our current physical life is temporal, a millisecond when compared to the eternal life we received with the gift of salvation. Our pursuits should be for things of eternal consequence, not temporal happiness.

Credit cards come to mind. You can make an immediate purchase, and get immediate gratification and happiness, but the end result is debt. And heavy debt makes us slaves. Another way to look at it is by considering those long-lasting light bulbs. You can buy a regular bulb for a relatively low price that will last for several months, or you can pay a bit more for one that will last for years. Don't you think you'd be better off initially spending the extra money for a quality bulb that will give you better results in the long run? In our spiritual pursuit the extra effort is worth the *longer-lasting results*. Therefore, our *main* focus and efforts should be on the things with long-lasting earthly or eternal significance, not the temporal comforts of this world.

Let's take a closer look at some important elements of this growth process toward finding earthly significance.

FIND A CHURCH

An essential element for Christian maturity is finding a community or fellowship of believers; a group of like-minded, supportive Christians, hungry to grow, learn, and enjoy rich relationships. *Fellowship* is the sharing of similar interests, ideas, or experiences. When we do this as Christians, we enjoy encouragement in our faith that takes us toward a more intimate relationship with God. Finding a church is *not* finding a building—it is finding people like you who are seeking to grow their relationships with God. Think of church as a fellowship of people you want to share part of your life with.

The early Christians sold all their possessions and pooled their resources in a sort of "communal living" arrangement. During this time, the Church experienced rapid growth. The Church's style and structure has changed over the years and will continue to change, but one thing is clear, finding a community of fellow believers isn't just a good idea, it's a *biblical* idea:

⊕ *And let us consider how we may spur one another on toward love and good deeds. Let us not give up meeting together...* (Hebrews 10:24-25).

When I say "like-minded" I don't mean that you need to find a group of people who think, look, or live just like you do. Some of our greatest spiritual growth comes from the interchange with other believers who have different life experiences and unique perspectives on living a life in the image and likeness of God. By like-minded I mean believers who are also seeking this and a deeper relationship with God. You might want to avoid people who believe they have already arrived at ultimate spirituality in their relationship with God. They will lack a certain amount of humility and hunger for a deeper relationship, both of which are important for you to see and copy.

A good church is a lot like a barbecue pit filled with hot coals. When you remove a coal from the pile it quickly cools. Find a good church to regularly attend and it will help keep the embers of your faith burning hot and vibrant.

Choosing a church can seem a daunting task. But it's important to take your time and find one that is a good fit for you—one where you can worship, learn, and grow in your faith. Do you have friends who go to church? Start your search there. Invite yourself to join them for one of their services. You might find a church that feels "right" on your very first visit. Or it could take weeks of searching. That's OK. Take the time you need. Church-shopping is fine when you're a new believer (or new to a community), but after you've found a good one, it's best to grow roots there. Frequent church-hopping or transplanting after you've started to settle in isn't conducive to spiritual growth. A church fellowship where others know you well can help you get the most out of your experience.

One of the first things you'll notice about churches is the diversity of worship styles. By "worship style" I'm referring to the part of the service where we sing to and about what God has done and is doing in our lives. You may feel most comfortable in a church that has a contemporary service, complete with a rock band, dynamic drama performances, and creative multimedia content. Or perhaps you'll be drawn to a more traditional service with hymns instead of modern choruses. As you will discover later in Book Two, worship is a very important part of developing a strong relationship with God, so your comfort level with worship is *very important*.

You'll find churches of all sizes, too. A small church might feel more like a "family" to you, while a larger church will likely provide more specialized teaching and ministry opportunities. No matter where you go, you're not going to find a community of perfect people. Churches are filled with sinners who are working on their spiritual lives just like you—a community working together toward spiritual growth. This includes the leadership of the church. While leaders have been given spiritual authority, they are still imperfect people working on their spiritual growth just as you are. God can only use imperfect people to build His Church, growing together in Him toward that goal of perfection. So be wise and *understanding* when it comes to the church family.

It's important to feel a sense of belonging wherever you end up. Look for people who are authentic about the ups and downs of their walk—ones you can be authentic with about yours. It's also critical to your growth to be challenged and have your faith stretched. Being comfortable with the teaching and the worship will make it easy to want to go to church—but being challenged by the teaching and inspired by the worship will make it worth the trip. You'll know when you've found the right one—stick with it even when the *inevitable* challenges arise.

ACTION & VISUALIZATION

Find a church or fellowship of Christians and attend regularly.

BAPTISM

After you've found a church that feels like a match, it's time to consider baptism. Just before He began His ministry, Jesus Himself was baptized (by John the Baptist). This shows us the importance of baptism. At the end of His ministry, Jesus commissioned His disciples to continue baptizing others:

✝ [Jesus said] *"Therefore go and make disciples of all the nations, baptizing them in the name of the Father and of the Son and of the Holy Spirit..."* (Matthew 28:19).

What is baptism? Essentially it is a public confession of a private decision. It is a way to identify with Jesus' death (going under the water) and resurrection (coming out of the water). It is a beautiful event that can be a powerful experience for you, and for those who are observing the public confession of your faith.

Baptism points us to one of the most significant aspects of our new lives in Christ—Jesus' resurrection, which is sometimes over shadowed by His death for our sins. Read what Paul says in Romans:

✝ *Or don't you know that all of us who were baptized into Christ Jesus were baptized into His death? We were therefore buried with Him through baptism into death in order that, just as Christ was **raised** from the dead through the glory of the Father, **we** too may live a **new life**. If we have been united with Him like this in His death, we will certainly also be **united with Him in His resurrection**. For we know that our old self was crucified with Him so that the body of sin might be done away with, that we should **no longer be slaves** to sin...* (Romans 6:3-6).

Jesus' death and resurrection gave us freedom from slavery to sin and are the mechanism that will one day give us complete freedom in Him. It is your choice to set this mechanism in motion by accepting Jesus' sacrifice on the Cross; however, you must also decide *daily* to *avoid* sin so that you can take advantage of *freedom from sin.*

Some theologians believe baptism is no more than a symbol of the inward change that happened the moment you accepted Christ as your

Savior. I believe Paul is suggesting that baptism actually plays a role in *creating* inward spiritual change. If nothing else, the courage it takes to publicly express your identification with Christ's death and resurrection certainly creates more of an *expectation* of change and freedom. Because we must choose daily to exercise that freedom, this *expectation* of change helps *make* those changes.

You will discover when we get to the gift of faith chapters that any action done in faith can have an impact in the spiritual world, and that in turn has an impact on the physical world. I believe the act of water baptism can in some ways help free you from slavery to sin or at least allow you to better exercise your freedom from it. Look at how Paul reinforces this concept:

✠ *...because anyone who has died has been freed from sin. Now if we died with Christ, we **believe** that we will also **live** with Him. For we know that since Christ was raised from the dead, He cannot die again; death no longer has mastery over Him. The death He died, He died to sin once for all; but the life He lives, He lives to God. In the same way, count* [baptize] *yourselves dead to sin but alive to God in Christ Jesus* (Romans 6:7-11).

During Christ's ministry and within the first-century church, the decision to accept Jesus as Savior and water baptism went hand in hand. When a person was saved, he was immediately baptized. In today's churches, it seems that more emphasis is placed on the verbal spiritual commitment. Our public expression of our faith commitment—baptism—is meant to occur in conjunction with the verbal spiritual commitment, representing the death of the old life and the resurrection into a new life in Christ. It is a symbol of what we are verbally confessing.

If you grew up in certain Christian denominations you may have been baptized as a baby or very young child. Obviously at the time you were not making a voluntary public identification with Jesus' death and resurrection. I believe God wants you to knowingly memorialize your relationship with Him.

✠ *Peter replied, "Repent and be baptized, every one of you, in the name of Jesus Christ"* (Acts 2:38).

Throughout the New Testament people were instructed to receive Christ and to be baptized as we see in this account when the Apostle Paul was saved.

✠ *[Ananias said] "And now what are you waiting for? Get up, be baptized and wash your sins away, calling on His name"* (Acts 22:16).

I encourage you to be baptized so the purpose of this water baptism can be fulfilled in your life. God is as excited about this decision as you are. Think about it!

ACTION & VISUALIZATION
Arrange with a pastor to be baptized.

CHANGE OLD HABITS

When you accept the gift of salvation, you are *changed*. Read what the apostle Paul says about this:

✠ *Therefore, if anyone is in Christ, he is a **new creation**; the old has gone, the new has come!* (2 Corinthians 5:17)

The word *new* in this passage is *kainos (kahee-noss),* which means unused, fresh, or novel. It's used here in regard to form and quality, rather than in reference to time (a thought conveyed by a similar-sounding word, *neos*). One of the Bible's wonderful, transforming truths is that Jesus offers everyone a chance to start over in life. No matter what you have done in the past or who you may have been, when you accept Jesus Christ—your past is forgiven. You become a brand-new person with a totally *new identity* in Him![1]

✠ *As far as the east is from the west, so far has He* [God] *removed our transgressions from us* (Psalm 103:12).

This change happens immediately—it's a heart change that occurs the moment you accept Jesus. But old *habits* die hard. Even though you may be a new creation in spirit, you continue to live in the old world and in your old body under the direction of a mind with old programming. To get the full effect of *all* the *freedoms* this first gift of life can bring, you will need to work at *re-programming* your mind and body. This is one of the main reasons to find a good church or fellowship. Here you can surround yourself with friends who are also striving to become a "new creation" and learning how to do that daily. It may be equally important to move away from some old friends—friends and habits that tie you to the old life. Here's what the Bible advises:

✠ *Blessed is the man who does **not** walk in the counsel of the wicked or stand in the way of sinners or sit in the seat of mockers* (Psalm 1:1).

✠ *He who walks with the wise grows wise, but a companion of fools suffers harm* (Proverbs 13:11).

✠ *Do not mislead: "bad company corrupts good character"* (1 Corinthians 15:33).

When you accepted Jesus you received your new insight—spiritual sight—which is dim at first. There is another story in the Bible of a blind man who was healed that presents interesting spiritual parallels for our stories:

✠ *They came to Bethsaida, and some people brought a blind man and begged Jesus to touch him. He took the blind man by the hand and **led him outside the village**. When He had **spit** on the man's eyes and put His hands on him, Jesus asked, "**Do you see anything?**" He looked up and said, "I see people; they look like trees walking around." Once more Jesus put His hands on the man's eyes. Then his eyes were opened, his sight was restored, and he saw everything clearly. Jesus sent him home, saying, "**Don't go into the village**"* (Mark 8:22-26).

Jesus first led the blind man outside the village. Your spiritual sight is a very personal thing between you and God. Without God, the world can't understand what you are now seeing. The next thing that happened would have been considered offensive by the world—Jesus spit on the man's eyes. The Gospel is likewise offensive to some and therefore they don't come to Jesus to get insight. Jesus then asks the blind man a question, "Do you see anything?" to which the man replied that he saw something, but not clearly. This is where we are now. We see something spiritually, yet not clearly. We now know we have an eternity within us, yet we don't see everything.

✠ *He [God] has made everything beautiful in its time. He has also set eternity in the hearts of men; yet they cannot fathom what God has done from the beginning to end* (Ecclesiastes 3:11).

Jesus continues to work with us, but we must choose to learn that which we do not know and to grow. It's a life long growth process. Jesus sends us home with the instruction not to go back into the world *for our sight.*

Take a moment to think about each of your current relationships. Do they encourage behaviors or actions that are contradictory to your new relationship with God? How wise would it be to continue those relationships? Remember how your computer (subconscious and central nervous system) works. When you see familiar faces and places your computer will automatically run old programs. The apostle Paul struggled with this very thing, too:

✞ *For I have the desire to do what is good, but I cannot carry it out. For what I do is not the good I want to do; no, the evil I do not want to do—this I keep on doing* (Romans 7:18-19).

Just like Paul, you will not always be able to stop old programs from running—programs that lead you into sin. You can make it easier on yourself by saying "no" to some of those old faces, places, and habits. Visualize yourself doing this. In time, with a regular commitment to positive influences, you'll develop new computer programs that avoid old patterns. In time, old programming will become obsolete and your new programming will allow you to shine God's light in those old dark places.

ACTION & VISUALIZATION

*Where necessary, avoid old friends and old places
that lead a new creation back to old habits.*

READ THE BIBLE

To continue on your journey toward spiritual growth, you need to know your history. The most important history you can know is "history" as in "His Story"—God's story, written in the Bible. God is part of your past, present, and future, so the Bible is also *your* story. It is life's ultimate direction manual for those who are serious about seeking wisdom.

✟ *I write these things to you who believe in the Name of the Son of God so that you may know that you have eternal life* (1 John 5:13).

✟ *...Always be prepared to give an answer to everyone...for the hope that you have...* (1 Peter 3:15).

The *B-I-B-L-E* is our "*Believers Instruction Book for Living on Earth.*" I recommend reading the Bible every day. You don't have to read dozens of chapters to get something valuable out of it. Sometimes a single verse can have a powerful impact on you. All Scripture has meaning on some level if you consider them carefully. As you study the Bible, read expectantly and look for ways you can apply the truths to your life. Here's another amazing thing about God's Book—you can read the same passage dozens of times and still find something new. God's Word is rich and alive!

✟ *For the Word of God is living and active. Sharper than any double-edged sword, it penetrates even to dividing soul and spirit, joints and marrow; it judges the thoughts and attitudes of the heart* (Hebrews 4:12).

Are you new to the Bible? Does the size of the Book, the tiny print, and the seemingly overwhelming amount of content intimidate you? Well, you're not alone. To make it easier, here's how it all breaks down. Basically, the Bible is divided into *two* parts, the Old and New Testaments. The Old Testament tells the story of the creation of the world and the history of God's interaction with the world until about 400 B.C. (before Christ). The books in the Old Testament, while important for their historical content and the unique stories they tell, also play a role in the foretelling of Jesus Christ's place in God's larger story. There are many specific prophecies in the Old Testament that accurately predicted the details of Jesus' life, along with many symbolic references in stories, events, and peoples' lives that predicted Jesus' ministry and purpose. Some of these predictions occurred more than a *thousand years before* Jesus' birth. *It's truly amazing!*

The "New Testament" tells the story of Jesus, who was the Messiah foretold by the Old Testament, and the story of the early Christian church. Until only recently, time was divided into two parts based on the life of Jesus (B.C.—before Christ, or A.D.—*anno domini* which means "the year of our Lord"). Peoples' lives have revolved around Jesus for over a thousand years whether they believe in Him or not. (Only recently it has become "politically correct" in the secular world to denote time periods with B.C.E.—Before Common Era, and C.E.—Common Era.)

The Old Testament may initially seem like stories of ancient people in another time that hold little relevance to your spirituality; however, as you develop your spiritual insight you will see that these people's stories can guide you in your spiritual walk. Paul, in writing about his Israelite forefathers from the time of Moses, said the following:

☦ *They were all baptized into Moses in the cloud and in the sea. They all ate the same spiritual food and drank the same spiritual drink; for they drank from the spiritual rock that accompanied them, and that rock was Christ. Nevertheless, God was not pleased with most of them; their bodies were scattered over the desert. **Now these things*** *occurred as examples to keep us from setting our hearts on evil things as they did* (1 Corinthians 10:2-6).

The Bible (from the Greek word *biblios*, meaning "book"), is made up of 66 smaller books written by 40 authors over 1,600 years. Although it was written over such a long period of time by different authors, all the books from Genesis, the first book, to Revelation, the last book, have a *consistent* and relevant message. This in and of itself is a *miracle*, showing the *divine hand of God* on its *writing*.

When you see a quote from the Bible, it is usually followed by a reference that identifies where you can find the quote. Just a side note—chapter and verse numbers were not part of the original writings, they were added to later translations for easier reference. I have included references throughout this book so you can go straight to the source and study the subject and context yourself.

Context is an important consideration when studying the Bible. As with any written work, simply pulling a sentence or two out of the whole can sometimes lead to an incorrect interpretation. Get to know the entire story, and each verse will make more sense.

You will want to choose a Bible that fits your reading style and level. There are many versions of the English Bible, some dating back hundreds of years. Since we don't use the same words as we did in 1700, it's usually a good idea to begin with a Bible that has been translated into modern English. The best way to choose a Bible is to go to a local *Christian* bookstore and invite a conversation with the Bible specialist. This person is familiar with the different versions of Bibles and can help you choose the one that best fits you.

The Bible is filled with God's very words to us—it is not just any old collection of writings. The ideas and the wisdom found in the Bible are to be taken, well, not like good advice, but as the words of your Creator! The Bible has this to say about that:

✠ *All Scripture is **God-breathed** and is useful for teaching, rebuking, correcting and training in righteousness* (2 Timothy 3:16).

✠ *Above all, you must understand that no prophecy of Scripture came about by the prophet's own interpretation. For prophecy never had its origin in the will of man, but men spoke from God as **they were carried along by the Holy Spirit*** (2 Peter 1:20-21).

We read the Bible because God asks us to. He wants us to get to know Him better. Knowledge of someone would be required to improve any relationship. The better we know and understand Him, the better friend we can be to Him. Jesus points out how important it is to learn and understand what God is doing so we can know how to be a true friend.

✠ *You are my friends if you do what I command. I no longer call you servants, because a servant does not know his master's business. Instead, I have called you friends, for everything that I learned from my Father I have made known to you* [to us through the Bible] (John 15:14-15).

And we read the Bible because it gives us great knowledge on how to live this life. The key is being diligent and open-minded when reading the Bible.

✠ *...seek and you will find...* (Matthew 7:7).

If you are reading God's living word with expectancy, diligence, and faith, then you will find something new every time you open your Bible. (We'll learn later how the Holy Spirit also helps us to get the most out of our Bible reading.) This new information will help reprogram your computer mind, establishing new habits. Choose a reading time and place you can return to regularly; however, I caution you not to develop your reading of the Bible into a mindless habit. Seek to keep it *fresh*. Supplement your Bible reading with other Christian reading material on subjects that interest you.

While the Bible has a beginning, middle, and end, it's not necessary to begin reading Genesis. I recommend starting at the Gospel of John in the New Testament, then read through to the end of Revelation. Beginning with John gives you the details of the life of Jesus, His ministry, death, and resurrection. Remember, this isn't a book you read once and put on the shelf—you'll come back to the Bible over and over again for the rest of your life. It is always *new* and *alive* for those who diligently seek the Truth.

✝ *Do not let this Book of the Law depart from your mouth; meditate on it day and night, so that you may be careful to do everything written in it* (Joshua 1:8).

ACTION & VISUALIZATION
Start reading your Bible daily.

TAKE COMMUNION

Jesus Himself asked us to participate in something called the Lord's Supper:

☩ *And He took bread, gave thanks and broke it, and gave it to them, saying, "This is My body given for you; do this in remembrance of Me." In the same way, after the supper He took the cup* [of wine], *saying, "This cup is the new covenant in My blood, which is poured out for you"* (Luke 22:19-20).

Many churches refer to this as "communion." It is a powerful place to meet God because it is a vivid reminder of Jesus' sacrifice on the Cross. While churches vary in how they present communion, you will find that most (if not all) place a high value on this experience. It's a time to reflect not only on Jesus' death, but also on our lives. We are asked to confess our sins before we come to the communion table. When we do approach the table to drink Jesus' blood (usually represented by grape juice or wine) and eat of His flesh (represented by bread), it is a solemn moment in which we can contemplate the significance of our *new* life in Jesus Christ and the promise of something wonderful—the joy of our salvation. Many people find that taking communion is a transcendent experience—a sacred place to meet God.

ACTION & VISUALIZATION

*Regularly participate in communion remembering
the sacrifice Jesus made for you.*

REMEMBER THE SABBATH

God set aside one day of the week for us to honor Him, to focus on the spiritual side of life and rest from our physical activities.

✠ *Remember the Sabbath day by keeping it holy. Six days you shall labor and do all your work, but the seventh day is a Sabbath to the Lord your God. On it you shall not do any work, neither you, nor your son or daughter, nor your manservant or maidservant, nor your animals, nor the alien within your gates. For in six days the Lord made the heavens and the earth, the sea, and all that is in them, but He rested on the seventh day. Therefore the Lord blessed the Sabbath day and made it holy* (Exodus 20:8-11).

✠ *And God blessed the seventh day and made it holy, because on it He rested from all the work of creating that He had done* (Genesis 2:3).

If you keep this day for rest and spiritual rejuvenation, you'll soon discover how it helps with both your spirit and attitude. Taking time to reflect on the spiritual things can also bless the other days of your week. The more you diligently follow this instruction, the more you will see His life-giving results in your life.

Consider these two principles regarding the day of rest. First, if you happen to have a job that requires you to work on Sunday, just choose another day of the week as your "Sabbath." The goal of Sabbath is rest and focus on God any day of the week, not adherence to a pointless religious exercise. Second, taking one day a week to rest and focus on spiritual things doesn't mean we are free to forget God on the other days of the week. The Christian life is a 24-7 proposition. Keeping the Sabbath gives us energy and wisdom and a rejuvenated spirit, making it easier to honor God with our words and actions the other six days of the week. It also gives us an opportunity to do some reprogramming through meditation and visualization.

Spiritually speaking, the number six represents the flesh of man so we exert our flesh in labor for six days. The number seven represents Heaven—which stands for perfection. In it you will obtain perfect rest.

ACTION & VISUALIZATION
Rest and honor God on the Sabbath.

REDEDICATE YOUR LIFE

If you already accepted the gift of salvation at some point in your life, but you drifted away from your relationship with Jesus, it's never too late to return. You might feel unworthy, like the first time you came to Him, but all that is asked of you is to repent of your sins—God is faithful to forgive.

✟ *If we confess our sins, He is faithful and just and will forgive us our sins and purify us from all unrighteousness* (1 John 1:9).

Because we're imperfect people—we still make bad choices, we still sin—we may find ourselves needing to return to Christ more than once over the course of our lives. We're in good company. Consider one of Jesus' disciples, Simon Peter, who was the first to identify Jesus as the Savior:

✟ *Simon Peter answered, "You are the Christ, the Son of the living God." Jesus replied, "Blessed are you, Simon son of Jonah, for this was not revealed to you by man, but by my Father in Heaven. And I tell you that you are Peter, and on this rock I will build my Church, and the gates of Hades will not overcome it* (Matthew 16:16-18).

This same person, as a solid follower of Christ, turned around and denied Jesus three times just prior to His death:

☩ *Now Peter was sitting out in the courtyard, and a servant girl came to him. "You also were with Jesus of Galilee," she said. But he denied it before them all. "I don't know what you're talking about," he said. Then he went out to the gateway, where another girl saw him and said to the people there, "This fellow was with Jesus of Nazareth." He denied it again, with an oath: "I don't know the man!" (Matthew 26:69-72).*

Sometimes the term *backsliding* is used to describe a time when people turn from their previously held views or direction. Simon Peter was the first to correctly identify Jesus as the Son of God, he served, lived with, and followed Jesus for three years—yet he denied Him three times.

But, here is the good news about Simon Peter's story (and ours as well): After Jesus rose from the dead, He came to Simon Peter and encouraged him, reaffirming His love, and sent him out to preach the Gospel with confidence. This renewed faith was underscored when Simon Peter spoke to a crowd (as recorded in the Book of Acts) and more than 5,000 people became believers as a result.

☩ *But many who heard the [Peter's] message believed, and the number of men grew to about 5,000 (Acts 4:4).*

If you have turned away from God for a season, Jesus knows your past; however, He is more interested in your future—in helping you fulfill your destiny. When you ask to be forgiven, He forgets all the stuff you did and welcomes you into His arms so that together you can look at where He wants you to walk next. He knows what you can be and what you can do if you align your will with His, because He is the One who can give you the power and ability if you allow Him.

If you need to come back to Jesus and repent, then say a prayer like this:

Father God I need to rededicate my life to You. I believe in my heart that Your Son, Jesus Christ, died to redeem me from my sins. I know I am a sinner and I ask You to forgive me. Help me to obey and follow You all the days of my life so that my life will be pleasing to You. I ask this in Jesus name, Amen.

DEVELOP AN ONGOING RELATIONSHIP

Whether you have prayed to receive the gift of salvation for the first time or have prayed a prayer of rededication—you have a relationship with Jesus. He wants to grow and expand this relationship at all times. Jesus said:

Here I am! I stand at the door and knock. If anyone hears My voice and opens the door, I will come in and eat with him, and he with Me (Revelation 3:20).

For many Christians, Revelation 3:20 is used to present the salvation message; however, in context Jesus is clearly speaking to people who are *already* Christians. He is saying that He wants to *build an intimate relationship with all believers.*

Dining with someone is a great setting to grow a relationship. Think about some of your best conversations—I'll bet many were shared across a table piled with food (whether in your kitchen, a restaurant, or sitting at a picnic table). A shared meal is a place of common ground, a welcoming place. Even business people use a shared meal to establish trust and build relationships. The Gospel of Luke (chapter 24) includes a story that illustrates the power of dining together.

Just after Jesus' resurrection, He comes across a couple of disciples walking along the road. They walk and talk with Him, but don't recognize Him as the Savior *until* they share a meal with Him. In the verse from Revelation, Jesus indicates His *readiness* and *desire* to have a deeper, more *intimate* relationship with us if we're *open* and *ready* to *receive* it.

What is important to God is *not* your position, power, or abilities—for all of those things come from Him. Nor is it your past—that's *behind* you. What is *most* important to God is developing a relationship with Him that *grows* with time. *Anyone* can grow closer by simply opening that door *whenever* He knocks. You must be listening and attentive to hear His knock.

There are many ways to welcome Him. I recommend simply being available to Him at all times. Don't limit your "God time" to praying before meals or before making important decisions; be open to God throughout your day, every day. This is what it means to have an attitude of prayer. The relationship God desires with you will open many opportunities during the day for the two of you to grow closer together.

ACTION & VISUALIZATION

Regularly seek more time to be with Jesus.

CONFORM YOUR IMAGE AND LIKENESS

As you seek a more intimate relationship with Jesus, you'll learn that He desires us to make certain changes to our lives. I have been asked by some Christians, "If I don't have to quit sinning to be accepted by God then why would I want to stop sinning at all?" It's actually a fair question. One answer is *gratitude* for God giving you eternal life and salvation.

✝ *Therefore, I urge you, brothers, **in view of God's mercy**, to offer your **bodies** as living sacrifices, holy and pleasing to God—this is your spiritual act of worship. Do not conform any longer to the pattern of this world, but be transformed by the renewing of your **mind**. Then you will be able to test and approve what God's will is—His good, pleasing and perfect will* (Romans 12:1-2).

These verses tell us that after we are saved, as an act of gratitude for eternal life, we conform our old bodies and minds to a new spirit. This is the process of working out our own salvation, which you read about previously.

A second reason for not sinning is because as a new creation, sinning goes against our new nature—it doesn't satisfy us anymore. As completely fallen people, we did completely fallen things and thought nothing of it. As born-again believers, we are completely different. Sure we can live in, and do often live in sin, but it's like a married man with another woman—he knows it's wrong, and will feel the weight of guilt until he makes it right.

The third reason is that this change is part of what it means to become Christlike. Because you are free, you can choose to fulfill the abundant life God intended for you. In the process of conforming yourself you will have to receive, unwrap, and use all the Gifts of Freedom God offers you. And ultimately, dwelling in His *image and likeness* is only accomplished when you are in an *intimate relationship* with Him. These go hand in hand. When I reference "image and likeness" I am also talking about this "most intimate relationship" and visa versa.

✝ *...and have put on the **new self**, which is being renewed in knowledge in the **image of its Creator*** (Colossians 3:10).

The fourth reason to avoid sin is that by living in His image and likeness in an intimate relationship with Him, you will certainly live an abundant life—experiencing all the things God intended for you.

Unfortunately, many Christians who receive the gift of salvation do not go on to receive, unwrap, or use all the additional gifts God offers. Some Christians don't pursue what it means to be Christlike, what it means to conform our image and likeness to Christ's, which means their intimacy with God suffers. Christians who diligently seek Christlikeness discover the amazing, supernatural ways God can meet them and help them grow. This is an important reason to avoid sin: to grow a closer, more intimate relationship with God. Dwelling in this place is to know a joyful life—more than you have ever experienced.

Pursuing Christlikeness is just what it sounds like—choosing daily to be like Jesus. Jesus is the living expression of all that God wants to communicate to us. Jesus was fully man (He walked this earth in a body like yours and mine). He was also fully God (He had the Spirit of God in Him). By God's intent, Jesus is the perfect model for us to observe, emulate, and conform to.

✟ *And just as we have borne the likeness of the earthly man* [Adam], *so shall we bear the likeness of the Man from Heaven* [Jesus] (1 Corinthians 15:49).

Jesus Himself said we should do as He does. After He demonstrated how to be a servant by washing His disciple's feet, Jesus said:

✟ *Now that I, your Lord and Teacher, have washed your feet, you also should wash one another's feet* (John 13:14).

Jesus wants you to use Him as a model as you seek to become more in the image and likeness of your Creator. God does not care what you look like on the outside or even about the good deeds you do to make yourself look good—deeds that are not coming from your heart. Jesus had this insiteful exchange with the religious leaders of the time.

✝ *Then some Pharisees and teachers of the law came to Jesus from Jerusalem and asked, "Why do your disciples break the tradition of the elders? They don't wash their hands before they eat!"* [A tradition set up that did not come from the Word of God or from the heart]. *Jesus replied, "And why do you break the command of God for the sake of your tradition? ...You hypocrites! Isaiah was right when he prophesized about you: 'These people honor Me with their lips, but their hearts are far from Me. They worship Me in vain; their teachings are but rules taught by men.'" Jesus called the crowd to Him and said, "Listen and understand. What goes into a man's mouth does not make him 'unclean,' but* **what comes out of his mouth, that is what makes him 'unclean'"** (Matthew 15:1-3,7-11).

God's desire is for us to begin remaking ourselves into His image and likeness starting with what He sees—the *inside.*

✝ *As water reflects a face, so a man's heart reflects the man* (Proverbs 27:19).

The road to becoming like Jesus is a lifelong one. Just look at what God says to Jesus after He was baptized (this was before Jesus started His ministry):

✝ *...You are my Son, whom I love; with you I am well pleased* (Luke 3:22).

What caused God to say He was so pleased with Jesus? At age 30, Jesus hadn't started His ministry. He hadn't saved one soul, healed one person, nor performed one miracle. An earlier verse in Luke tells us:

✚ *And Jesus grew in wisdom and stature, and in favor with God and men* (Luke 2:52).

Jesus had been *preparing* Himself to fulfill God's plan for His life; *increasing* in knowledge and wisdom, *learning* from Scripture, and *growing closer to His Father through prayer.* This is where you are, too—*preparing yourself* so you will fulfill God's will for your life—growing *closer* so you can be used by Him.

As unique individuals, each of us has a *different* purpose in life which leads us to our personalized abundant life once fulfilled; however, to fulfill our noble purposes we must prepare ourselves first by being born again, then by seeking to conform ourselves to His image and likeness.

✚ *In a large house there are articles not only of gold and silver, but also of wood and clay; some are for noble purposes and some for ignoble. If a man cleanses himself from the latter, he will be an instrument for noble purposes, made holy, useful to the Master and prepared to do any good work. Flee the evil desires of youth, and pursue righteousness, faith, love and peace, along with those who call on the Lord out of a pure heart* [other like-minded believers] (2 Timothy 2:20-22).

Conforming to the likeness of Christ will build up and strengthen your spiritual life which will be necessary for you to fully achieve your unique purpose in life and the abundant life that comes with it. You are a human *being* not a human *doing*—God is most interested in who you are, not what you do. If you take time to prepare your heart and strengthen your spiritual relationship with Him—God will be close to you. That's not to say that He will not want you to act a certain way, to preach or teach or share the Gospel message with others—but *who* you *are* is most important. This will ultimately determine *what* you *do* as God guides you *personally.*

There is an order to this process. It's like when you get on a plane and the flight attendant tells parents, "in the event of an emergency, secure your oxygen mask before your children's." This is because the chance for survival is much greater if the parent cares for themselves first. We need to *prepare ourselves first* so we are *able* to help others.

Jesus demonstrated a life of servanthood for us to follow, as exemplified in washing His disciples' feet. This is an important aspect of spiritual growth, seeking to help and serve others. Helping others brings you closer to God and therefore spiritual growth occurs. But Jesus also withdrew from the crowds and people in need at times and spent time alone in prayer, renewing Himself with God.

Remember, God is more interested in growing you from the inside out—which happens in solitude through listening, study, and prayer. So don't ever let "doing a bunch of Christian activities" distract you from your priority—developing your spiritual relationship with God. This can be a difficult and delicate balancing act at times, as you will also want to grow as a servant, too.

Jesus' life was a perfect example for us to follow. The degree to which we can follow in His footsteps is the degree we can live a powerful, *supernatural, spirit-filled life* and have a significant *impact* on the world as you become *like* Him and become His *evidence* in the world:

For you were once darkness, but now you are light in the Lord. Live as children of light (Ephesians 5:8).

✝ *You* [Christians] *are the light of the world. A city on a hill cannot be hidden. Neither do people light a lamp and put it under a bowl. Instead they put it on its stand, and it gives light to everyone in the house. In the same way, let your light shine before men, that they may see your good deeds* [actions in the will of God] *and praise* [or come to know] *your Father in Heaven* [because they are seeing Him in *you*] (Matthew 5:14-16).

We begin our relationship with God by identifying ourselves with Jesus' death and resurrection. We then must diligently conform ourselves to His image and likeness in all aspects of our lives as we grow our relationship with Him by receiving, unwrapping, and using additional Gifts of Freedom. While the apostle Paul says we will never fully achieve perfection in this life, it should be our aim.

✝ *Aim for perfection, listen to my appeal, be of one mind, live in peace. And the God of love and peace will be with you* (2 Corinthians 13:11).

If we want to follow God, then we are called to model our lives after His beloved Son.

✝ *For those God foreknew* [you] *He also predestined to be conformed to the likeness of his Son, that He* [Jesus] *might be the Firstborn among many brothers* (Romans 8:29).

ACTION & VISUALIZATION
Conform yourself to the image and likeness of Jesus Christ.

MEDITATION POINT

Follow in His steps.

Go to Chapter 3 in the Study Guide section on page 281.

ENDNOTE

1.   Jack Hayford, ed. *Spirit Filled Life Bible for Students* (Nashville, TN: Thomas Nelson Publishers, 1995), 1502.

Chapter 4

GIFT #2—THE HOLY SPIRIT (PART 1)
WHAT DOES THE HOLY SPIRIT MEAN IN YOUR LIFE?

Before you begin to read, pray that the Holy Spirit
will give you understanding and application.

✠ *Peter replied, "Repent and be baptized, every one of you, in the name
of Jesus Christ for the forgiveness of your sins. And you will receive the
gift of the **Holy Spirit** (Acts 2:38).*

THE HOLY SPIRIT AND YOU

When you fell in love with your husband or wife you probably couldn't wait to introduce them to your friends and family. This person was so wonderful you just had to share him or her with others—you couldn't keep this gift to yourself. When Jesus was departing the world and introduced it to the Holy Spirit, it was much the same. Jesus was saying, "Yes, you know and have seen Me, but though I am leaving, just wait until you meet this wonderful Counselor, Guide, and Helper—the Holy Spirit."

✠ *I will not leave you as orphans... (John 14:18).*

Jesus' promise was fulfilled by the next Gift of Freedom: the *Holy Spirit*.

✠ *And I will ask the Father, and He will give you another Counselor to be with you forever...* (John 14:16).

When Jesus promised the coming of the Holy Spirit to believers, what He was promising was a new connection with God, a gift for those who would believe:

✠ [Jesus said] *"When the **Counselor** comes, Whom I will send to you from the Father, the Spirit of truth who goes out from the Father, He will testify about Me"* (John 15:26).

✠ [Jesus said to His disciples] *"Now I am going to Him who sent Me... It is for your good that I am going away. Unless I go away, the **Counselor** will not come to you; but if I go, I will send Him to you"* (John 16:5,7).

✠ *By this He meant the **Spirit**, Whom those who believed in Him were later to receive. Up to that time the **Spirit** had not been given, since Jesus had not yet been glorified* (John 7:39).

I imagine you may be feeling a bit overwhelmed right about now. Perhaps you're wondering how you can absorb all of these new thoughts, feelings, and information. Perhaps you're asking, "What else do I need to know?" "How will I apply all of these new concepts to my daily life?" "How do I go about making necessary life changes (especially difficult ones)?" Rest assured, these questions are familiar to most new believers—I asked them myself after I accepted the first gift of salvation. The all-encompassing simple answer to these questions is the *Holy Spirit,* which is a gift you *automatically* receive when you *accept* the gift of life.

WHO IS THE HOLY SPIRIT?

Before we see how the Holy Spirit is going to help you, let's understand who He is and where He came from. The Holy Spirit was present at the creation of the world:

Now the earth was formless and empty, darkness was over the surface of the deep, and the Spirit of God was hovering over the waters (Genesis 1:2).

Then God said, "Let Us [the Father, the Son, and the Holy Spirit] *make man in our image, in our likeness..."* (Genesis 1:26).

The Holy Spirit is an important part of the Holy Trinity. Jesus said:

The Spirit gives life... (John 6:63).

Elsewhere in Scripture, this theme of life is repeated:

The Spirit of God has made me; the breath [Spirit] *of the Almighty gives me life* (Job 33:4).

The Holy Spirit also was involved in the creation of Jesus' human life:

✝ *This is how the birth of Jesus Christ came about: His mother Mary was pledged to be married to Joseph, but before they came together, she was found to be with child through the Holy Spirit* (Matthew 1:18).

And the Holy Spirit brings Jesus to life after his death on the Cross:

✝ *For Christ died for sins once for all, the righteous for the unrighteous, to bring you to God. He was put to death in the body but made alive by the Spirit..."* (1 Peter 3:18).

✝ *And if the Spirit of Him Who raised Jesus from the dead is living in you, He Who raised Christ from the dead will also give life to your mortal bodies through His Spirit, Who lives in you* (Romans 8:11).

And finally, when *you* become a new Christian—born again—God gives you a new heart and a regenerated spirit as well as the Holy Spirit to guide you.

✝ *I* [God] *will give you a new heart and put a new spirit in you; I will remove from you your heart of stone and give you a heart of flesh. And I will put my Spirit in you and move you to follow My decrees and be careful to keep My laws* (Ezekiel 36:26-27).

FOR EVERY CHRISTIAN

Jesus promises *every* Christian the indwelling power of the Holy Spirit, to lead and reveal God's truth within you. Remember what I said earlier about the Holy Trinity? God is made up of three Persons: God the Father, Jesus the Son, and the Holy Spirit. The word used in the original text to refer to the Holy Spirit is *parakletos (par-ak-lay-toss)*. *Parakletos* comes from the word *para*, which means "beside," and *kaleo*, which means "to call." Together they suggest someone called to one's side. The word signifies a comforter, a helper, an advocate and a *counselor*, as Jesus described. In non-biblical literature the word *parakletos* often referred to an attorney, someone who would appear in court on another's behalf.[1]

The Holy Spirit helps us in a number of key ways. He leads believers to a greater understanding of Gospel truths, gives us strength to endure the hostility of the world, and helps us communicate with God.

"For My thoughts are not your thoughts, neither are your ways My ways," declares the Lord. "As the heavens are higher than the earth, so are My ways higher than your ways and My thoughts than your thoughts" (Isaiah 55:8-9).

We can't understand the ways and nature of God because we have been shaped by earthly circumstances. Our minds have been, in a sense, grounded, and that grounding leads us to death or a disconnection with God. Still, we desperately need a way to communicate with God. Our earthly bodies and minds block us from intimacy with a holy, sinless God. The Holy Spirit helps us connect to God's ways—which are unreachable on our own.

Read what else Jesus said of the Holy Spirit:

*And I will ask the Father, and He will give you another Counselor to be with you forever—the Spirit of truth. The world cannot accept Him, because it neither sees Him nor knows Him. But you know Him, for He lives **with** you and will be **in** you* (John 14:16-17).

When you are born again the Holy Spirit becomes your companion for life, literally dwelling within you. The moment you accept the gift of salvation, you receive a gift the world doesn't have: a comforter and counselor you can call on to help you face life's many challenges, the Holy Spirit.

☩ *As for you, the anointing* [Holy Spirit] *you received from Him remains in you, and you do not need anyone to teach you, but as His anointing teaches you about all things and as that anointing is real, not counterfeit—just as it has taught you, remain in Him* (1 John 2:27).

The Helper or Anointing can show you truth when the world offers lies and uncertainty.

How does the Holy Spirit bring you to truth? How can you listen and follow the Spirit in your life? You have to be receptive to the Holy Spirit speaking to you through your spirit. He will speak to you through other people; He will speak to you through events and circumstances. Become sensitive to the Holy Spirit's communications with you and reprogram yourself to receive them by consciously opening your mind and spirit to Him—become childlike.

Remember how you programmed yourself to drive? Your eyes and mind learned to pick out important information as you drove: the red or green traffic lights, the red octagonal sign, and countless other traffic instructions, not to mention other vehicles, street signs, roadwork, etc. Now you process this information automatically, without conscious thought, right? It has become second nature. We've reprogrammed our minds and bodies to detect, think, react, and process data as drivers.

Similarly, will you program your mind and body to detect, think, react, and process the Holy Spirit's active voice and signs put in your life as a Christian seeking a deeper relationship with God?

✝ *When He* [the Holy Spirit] *comes, He will convict the world of guilt in regard to sin and righteousness and judgment* (John 16:8).

If we do not program ourselves to recognize these signs or choose *not* to follow them once detected, we're like a reckless driver behind the wheel. Our lives become chaotic with potentially devastating results, giving new meaning to the term, "hell on wheels." The Holy Spirit not only gives us divine insight to help us avoid unnecessary trouble in our lives, He also is our Guide, drawing us back toward the image and likeness of God.

Without the Holy Spirit, we, with our own ability, are *powerless to change.* Changing into His image and likeness can only happen by the guidance and through the *power* of the Holy Spirit—we need to accept His leading and power. And of course the complete fulfillment of this change will occur solely by Him in the next life. But, we can still discover what this means for us in our earthly lives; the degree to which we follow the Holy Spirit's lead determines how far we get toward our goal here on earth of being transformed to God's image and likeness.

✝ *Now the Lord is the Spirit, and **where the Spirit of the Lord is**, there is **freedom**. And we, who with unveiled faces all reflect the Lord's glory, are being transformed into His likeness with ever-increasing glory, which comes from the Lord, who is the Spirit* (2 Corinthians 3:17-18).

We are profoundly changed when we unite ourselves with the Spirit of God who gives us the *freedom* to change in ways you can't fully imagine right now. Assuming of course you *choose* to change. Read what the apostle Paul wrote to the church in Corinth:

✛ *But he who unites himself with the Lord is one with Him in spirit …Do you not know that your body is a temple of the Holy Spirit, Who is in you, Whom you have **received** from God?…* (1 Corinthians 6:17,19).

This does not mean, of course, that we become Jesus, or that we become God. But because of the Holy Spirit dwelling in us, we have access to all three aspects of the Holy Trinity. We have Jesus within us. We have God within us, which allows us the right to be called children of God and joint heirs with Christ for what our heavenly Father owns.

✛ *Because you are sons, God sent the Spirit of his Son **into our hearts**, the Spirit who calls out, "Abba, Father." So you are no longer a slave, but a son; and since you are a son, God has made you also an heir* (Galatians 4:6-7).

✛ *Now if we are children, then we are heirs—heirs of God and **co-heirs with Christ**, if indeed we share in His suffering in order that we may also share in His glory* (Romans 8:17).

What does it mean to be an heir of God? Under the Mosaic law—the law of the Old Testament—a father's property was divided among the sons of his legitimate wives. Succession to property was a matter of *right* and *not favor*. The Bible says Jesus Christ, God's begotten Son, is the "heir of all things" and that Christ-followers are "joint heirs with Christ". Yes, as a believer, a child of God, there will come a day when you will share in all things.

ACTION & VISUALIZATION

Consider your new standing with God and how that will affect your life.

MORE THAN BEFORE

This brings us to a most important point—now that you're a Christian, you are *more* than you were *before*. Read that again and remember it. You are a child of God, an heir to the King of kings.

We have already read that the Holy Spirit is the same Spirit who raised Jesus from the dead and gave Him life. *This same Spirit within you becomes part of your new identity.* God wants us to listen to the Spirit within us. Before you were a Christian, you primarily listened to the desires of your mind and the needs and wants of your body. But as a Christian, our real power doesn't come from our minds or our bodies, it comes from the Holy Spirit. As we restrain our minds and bodies and offer ourselves up to the *leading* and *shaping* of the Holy Spirit, we are *bringing* the Kingdom of Heaven within us. This is the place where Jesus Christ can take His place as King of your life.

Read what the apostle Paul wrote in Romans:

☩ *And if the Spirit of Him Who raised Jesus from the dead is living in you, He Who raised Christ from the dead will also give life to your mortal bodies through His Spirit, Who lives in you* (Romans 8:11).

Are you wrestling with an issue in your life that seems dead and hopeless? If so, remember that the same Spirit who raised Christ from the dead can provide you resurrection power in all parts of your life. Whether you need a physical, mental, social, or financial resurrection, your reliance on God is your only hope. His workspace is faith; this is where He can shape a fulfilling life for you. It also provides a forum where He can hear and respond to your desires. Your mind will put *limits* on what you can do, but God's will for your life is *limitless*. Connect yourself to God's Spirit in a meaningful relationship and watch your new identity start falling into place.

✠ *Flesh gives birth to flesh, but the Spirit gives birth to spirit* (John 3:6).

The Holy Spirit is a life-giving power.

✠ *The Spirit himself testifies with our spirit that we are God's children* (Romans 8:16).

While we have a new spirit, we're much like children. We have a lot to learn. We need a teacher, someone to instruct us in this new life as God's children. We need someone to help us change all our old programming. Who better than God to teach us? Remember Romans 12:1-2 says God wants us to realign our minds and bodies with His will so His will and purpose can be completed in our lives, and indeed through us into the world. He has given us the Holy Spirit to help teach, lead, and empower us to do that.

ACTION & VISUALIZATION

Consider how the Holy Spirit can change your identity.
You need to visualize and embrace the change
before you can fully benefit from your new identity.

THE POWER OF THE SPIRIT

Being in sync with God will put His power in sync with our efforts like a plane or kite uses the wind to achieve its goal of flight. The Holy Spirit can lift us to do God's will so we can soar in this life. This power allows you to accomplish things you could not accomplish otherwise: blessings, long life, benefits for your descendants, a closer relationship with God and much more.

✠ *All these blessings will come upon you and accompany you if you obey the Lord your God...You will be* **blessed when you come in** *and* **blessed when you go out** (Deuteronomy 28:2,6).

✠ *See that what you have heard from the beginning remains in you. If it does, you also will remain in the Son and in the Father* (1 John 2:24).

✠ *And if you walk in My ways and obey My statutes and commands as David your father did, I will give you a long life* (1 Kings 3:14).

✠ *Oh, that their hearts would be inclined to fear Me and keep all My commands always, so that it might go well with them and their children forever!* (Deuteronomy 5:29)

✠ *Now if you obey Me fully and keep My covenant, then out of all nations you will be My treasured possession...* (Exodus 19:5).

✠ *But seek first His Kingdom and His righteousness and all these things* [your needs] *will be given to you as well* (Matthew 6:33).

✠ *...because those who are led by the Spirit of God are sons of God* (Romans 8:14).

This is exciting stuff—but what does it take to get into alignment with God's will? How do we get into sync? We *begin* by understanding how the Holy Spirit works!

✠ *But the Counselor, the Holy Spirit, whom the Father will send in My name, will teach you all things and will remind you of everything I have said to you* (John 14:26).

✠ *You gave Your good Spirit to instruct them…*(Nehemiah 9:20).

✠ *…I will put My law in their minds and write it on their hearts. I will be their God, and they will be My people* (Jeremiah 31:33).

✠ *As for you, the anointing* [Holy Spirit] *you received from Him remains in you, and you do not need anyone to teach you. But as His anointing teaches you about all things and as that anointing is real, not counterfeit—just as it has taught you, remain in Him* (1 John 2:27).

When you read the Bible, you should always pray and invite the Holy Spirit to reveal spiritual and practical life application. The Holy Spirit illuminates truth which we are often too blind to see.

✠ *The man without the Spirit does not accept the things that come from the Spirit of God, for they are **foolishness** to him, and he **cannot understand** them, because they are **spiritually** discerned* (1 Corinthians 2:14).

The Holy Spirit sheds spiritual light and understanding, giving us revelation that could only be seen with His help. What He has revealed to you is supernatural and not understandable by the human mind. This is why it may seem crazy to your non-believing friends or family members.

✝ *For the message of the cross is **foolishness to those who are perishing**, but to **us** who are being saved it is the **power of God*** (1 Corinthians 1:18).

After I became a Christian, my unsaved friends accused me of being brainwashed when I spoke to them about my newfound belief. I told them, "I'm glad you noticed…because my brain *did* need washing." Of course, it was the Holy Spirit who did this cleansing.

The Holy Spirit teaches us and reveals God's laws or His ways of guiding us morally and spiritually. This allows us to use the *power* of these laws for our benefit and, of course, avoid being harmed. As an example adhering to the law of sowing and reaping will allow you to use its power to better reap the things you want in life and better avoid the things you don't.

The Holy Spirit also imprints these laws on our mind and heart to help us adjust to our new spirit:

✝ *The Holy Spirit also testifies to us about this. First He says: "This is the covenant I will make with them after that time, says the Lord. I will put My laws in their hearts, and I will write them on their minds"* (Hebrews 10:15-16).

To accomplish God's overall mission for us, the Bible says that the Holy Spirit's presence is everywhere:

✟ *Where can I go from Your Spirit? Where can I flee from Your presence? If I go up to the heavens, You are there; if I make my bed in the depths, You are there. If I rise on the wings of the dawn, if I settle on the far side of the sea, even there Your hand will guide me, Your right hand will hold me fast* (Psalm 139:7-10).

The Holy Spirit leads us into the completely fulfilling life God offers to all of His children. There may be times when we make some wrong turns from God's plan for our lives, but just like the new guidance systems on cars, the Holy Spirit is ever present, ready to get us back on track when *we're* ready again to follow His leading. This is important: You will make some wrong turns in this new life, but even then you won't be left alone without guidance. Even when you feel down or sad or like you've failed, the Holy Spirit is working to restore you just like your body does in such a marvelous way when you cut yourself.

✟ *We know that we live in Him and He in us, because He has given us of His Spirit* [Holy Spirit]. *And we have seen and testify that the Father has sent His Son to be the Savior of the world. If anyone acknowledges that Jesus is the Son of God, God lives in him and he in God* (1 John 4:13-15).

Paul, when explaining God to the Romans, says God had created and arranged everything in such a way that we might seek Him.

✟ *God did this so that men would seek Him and perhaps reach out for Him, though He is not far from each of us* (Acts 17:27).

ACTION & VISUALIZATION

Look and listen for the leading of the Holy Spirit in your life.

PROMPTED BY THE HOLY SPIRIT

When I became a Christian, I didn't know any other Christians, so there wasn't anyone who told me to "read the Bible." Instead, I was prompted by the Holy Spirit. The Holy Spirit also testified to me that the Bible is indeed the inspired Word of God—that all truth in the Bible was given by God. However, as I began reading, I discovered many difficult concepts that my natural mind could not fully understand. Sometimes, I didn't have someone to help me comprehend, so I would simply pray for the Spirit to help. Sure enough, something would happen to illuminate the Bible passage—whether it came through the sermon that week or a life experience. God has regularly used and still does use circumstances to teach me, bringing understanding when there seemingly was none.

When you prepare to read the Bible, ask the Holy Spirit to shed light on truth. Guidance from the Holy Spirit, however, is *not* limited to reading the Bible. Ask Him to illuminate truth in every circumstance and in all of life's situations. You will find truth as you read, and keep your eyes open long after you've closed your Bible—look for God's truth in everyday life.

There were times when I didn't hear God's voice clearly in my reading or even soon thereafter. But even on those occasions I received a confirmation in my spirit that I was not ready to understand. The process of spiritual growth is like that of physical or mental development. We're just not meant to understand everything from "day one." For instance, it would be pointless to discuss the relative educational merits of attending UCLA or Harvard with a 2-year-old. But when that toddler matures and is a student in high school, then yes, that student could understand conversation regarding higher education. Likewise, we grow in understanding as we grow closer to God.

Remember what Jesus said to His disciples:

✟ *I have much more to say to you, more than you can **now** bear* (John 16:12).

God packages and times His information when we are actually ready for it and truly capable of understanding and using it. We must be open and look for it though. This is why Jesus spoke in parables much of the time. Those whose hearts were open and eager for the truth would understand.

✟ [Jesus said] *"This is why I speak to them in parables: Though seeing, they do not see; though hearing, they do not hear or understand. In them is fulfilled the prophecy of Isaiah: 'You will be ever hearing but never understanding, you will be ever seeing but never perceiving. For this people's heart has become calloused; they hardly hear with their ears, and they have closed their eyes. Otherwise they might see with their eyes, hear with their ears, understand with their hearts and turn, and I would heal them'"* (Matthew 13:13-15).

An open heart assists our growing relationship with God which enables us to *understand* the spiritual things we see and hear. That maturity as Christians and the process of developing spiritual muscle and growth is expressed this way in Hebrews:

✟ *We have much to say about this, but it is hard to explain because you are slow to learn. In fact, though by this time you ought to be teachers, you need someone to teach you the elementary truths of God's word all over again. You need milk, not solid food! Anyone who lives on milk, being still an infant, is not acquainted with the teaching about righteousness. But solid food is for the mature, who by constant use have trained themselves to distinguish good from evil* (Hebrews 5:11-14).

The book you're holding is filled with a variety of foods—some milk and lots of meat. It's OK if you don't understand everything right away. Perhaps the next time you pick up this book you'll find a truth you didn't see the first time. Of course you should be reading and re-reading the Bible as often as you can. Each time you read the Bible the Holy Spirit will give you new understanding. Consistent study of God's teaching will help you better distinguish between good and evil.

ACTION & VISUALIZATION

Read the Bible daily and study other Christian resources often.
Expect the Holy Spirit to reveal fresh truth when you
keep your eyes and heart open.

ALL IN GOD'S TIME AND WAY

Sometimes God chooses to withhold information to protect us. He did this with the Israelites when they were escaping from Egypt.

When Pharaoh let the people go, God did not lead them on the road through the Philistine country, though that was shorter. For God said, "If they face war, they might change their minds and return to Egypt." So God led the people around by the desert road toward the Red Sea... (Exodus 13:17-18).

God always does things the *right* way—His loving way. And that's not always the quickest way or the way we might think is most logical. The Israelites, having just been freed from a long period of captivity, didn't have enough faith to face the enemy—the enemy they would have to fight to possess the Promised Land. At that point, God knew that they were spiritually underdeveloped—weak in faith they would be fearful and run back to Egypt—even if that meant back into slavery. Of course, they would ultimately have to battle the Philistines to obtain possession of the Promised Land, but God nurtured and matured their faith over time.

New and even us maturing Christians are a lot like these recently freed Israelites, still in need of nurturing. As with music, comedy, sports, and many other things in life, timing is *important* and God's plan is all about timing. God has *perfect* timing. The more you grow in faith, the more you'll learn to trust in *His perfect timing.*

ACTION & VISUALIZATION

Pray that the Holy Spirit will reveal things you
don't understand in your life.

BE OPEN TO ANSWERS YOU DON'T EXPECT

If you pray for revelation you will receive answers when God determines you are ready for them. When you ask for answers, ask with confidence and expectancy that the Holy Spirit will reveal truth, but also with the understanding that God sometimes answers in surprising, unexpected ways. Do not be overly influenced by what you *want* or *think* should happen.

Perhaps you've heard this little story that illustrates this point: once there was a Christian man whose neighborhood was flooding. He prayed and asked God to save him and God assured him He would. As the waters rose, a fire truck came by and the firemen offered the man a ride out of the neighborhood. The man was convinced God would save him so he said "No thanks." As the waters continued to rise, the man had to climb up onto his roof. A boat came by and offered him a ride. Still trusting God, he again replied, "No thanks." The flood kept rising and the man found himself balanced on his chimney, the water now moving up around his neck. A helicopter dropped a rope ladder and offered a flight to safety. With his faith still strong, the man said "No thanks, God is going to save me." Well, the waters didn't stop and the man finally drowned. When he got to Heaven he immediately went to God to complain, "I thought you said you were going to save me! What happened?" To that God replied "I sent a fire truck, a boat and a helicopter—what else did you expect Me to do?"

We need to be open, sensitive to God's answers so we can recognize them when they come. Unfortunately, sometimes we have to be hit over the head before we're ready to hear God. I can assure you, it is a lot easier when you get in tune with God's still, soft voice and learn to recognize Him and the signs He leaves you during life's circumstances. With time, study, prayer, and the guidance of the Holy Spirit, you can get better and better at hearing His voice and finding Him in the midst of troubling circumstances. Like so much of our faith, this too is a growth process.

Here's a story that has helped me understand this idea:

✠ *Now Moses was tending the flock of Jethro his father-in-law, the priest of Midian, and he led the flock to the far side of the desert and came to Horeb, the mountain of God. There the angel of the Lord appeared to him in flames of fire from within a bush. Moses saw that though the bush was on fire it did not burn up. So Moses thought, "I will go over and see this strange sight—why the bush does not burn up." When the Lord saw that he had **gone over to look**, God called to him from within the bush, "Moses! Moses!"… (Exodus 3:1-4).*

This story begins with Moses going about his daily work of shepherding. But in the middle of that typical day, he sees something unusual. Having an *inquisitive* and *open* spirit he takes a *closer* look. Here's the part I like best: it's only *after* God sees he is taking a closer look that He speaks to Moses. That last sentence could almost be rewritten like this: "When the Lord saw that Moses had gone to take a closer look for Him *in the circumstance,* that's when He chose to speak to Moses!" You will have to take a closer look at the circumstances in your life so you don't *just see,* but also *perceive* God's voice speaking to you through those circumstances.

Somewhere in the middle of your day, the Holy Spirit might be trying to get your attention. When we're open to taking a closer look, God can, and does, speak to us through circumstances. If we don't take a closer look, sometimes the Holy Spirit will diligently repeat the clues until we *do* hear Him. If you've been getting the same message over and over, it is possible God is trying to get your attention. Look for Him there.

Jesus scolded His disciples when they repeatedly missed the signs:

Aware of their discussion, Jesus asked them: "Why are you talking about having no bread? Do you still not see or understand? Are your hearts hardened? Do you have eyes but fail to see, and ears but fail to hear? And don't you remember?" (Mark 8:17-18)

The word for *hardened* in this passage, *poroo* (po-rah-oh), means "to petrify" or "to form a callous." It was sometimes used metaphorically to refer to spiritual deafness and blindness. Jesus was making the point that those who hear the Gospel and repeatedly resist its truth soon become insensitive and numb to the power of real understanding. Sinful lifestyles, false sophistication, intellectual pride, and self-reliance can also harden a heart toward the kind of truth the Holy Spirit brings.[2] Sins we repeat can make us callous, as we repeatedly ignore the Holy Spirit's urging to do otherwise. We, in essence, program ourselves to tune out the signs and therefore they will become of no benefit to us.

Our environment and experiences also condition us to automatically act and react in a certain, often God-less way. Influences such as our race, parents, upbringing, education, physical abilities, size, mental abilities, economic standing—each of these impact the way we think. But with salvation and the Holy Spirit's guidance and power, we can have real impact in the world beyond our life's experiences and influences.

The changes I have seen in my own life and in the lives of other believers are dramatic, even unbelievable considering our human abilities. Miraculous freedoms from bondages, physical and/or emotional healings, supernatural favor, and God's power and presence in you can completely reshape your story if you are open to it. *I know now that all things are possible with God,* by seeking, unwrapping, and using His life-changing *gifts.* God has much He would like to tell you and many gifts He would like to give you. It is the Holy Spirit who delivers or reveals God's gifts at His appointed time. Question: will you have your eyes and arms open when those times come?

However, as it is written: "No eye has seen, no ear has heard, no mind has conceived what God has prepared for those who love Him"—but God has revealed it to us by His Spirit. The Spirit searches all things, even the deep things of God. For who among men knows the thoughts of a man except the man's spirit within him? In the same way no one knows the thoughts of God except the Spirit of God. We have not received the spirit of the world but the Spirit who is from God, **that we may understand what** [gifts] **God has freely given us.** *This is what we speak, not in words taught us by human wisdom but in words taught by the Spirit, expressing spiritual truths in spiritual words* (1 Corinthians 2:9-13).

The Holy Spirit will teach us and confirm to our spirit all the spiritual laws of nature along with an understanding of the gifts God offers should we choose to receive, unwrap, and use them. The offer and receiving is done through God's *Spirit* to your spirit, so be attentive and listen.

ACTION & VISUALIZATION

*Be open and ready for truth, and answers
beyond your current expectations.*

SEEKING DIRECTION

Beyond an openness to God, it's beneficial to *actively seek* direction from the Holy Spirit in both the small and big decisions you face. Consider this passage from the Old Testament Book of Judges:

✝ *In those days Israel had no king; everyone did as he saw fit* (Judges 21:25).

Does this sound familiar? Apart from a relationship with God, people set their own standards of right and wrong. They are not basing these standards on God's perfect absolute truth, but instead on relative standards—standards that teach that most anything is OK depending on the circumstances. This approach didn't work for the Israelites; instead chaos and disaster ruled because it led them down the wrong path, a direction God did not want them to go. The same is still true today. However, as a follower of King Jesus, we can overcome this chaos in our life, and with the Holy Spirit's help, we can keep Jesus on the throne at the center of our lives.

The Holy Spirit also helps you choose the right paths to take in life–even when the road forks. He leads us down the path to *abundant life*.

I want to clarify that an abundant life does not necessarily mean riches, perfect health, no disappointments, and so on. An *abundant life* is when you achieve the things you were uniquely *destined by God* to achieve— being in the center of His will allow you to experience the fullest life possible for you to achieve.

There is no greater joy in life than to know and live out the experiences and achievements you were uniquely designed and destined for. Let me say again, reaching that destiny usually involves pain and struggle. The heroes, prophets, apostles, and disciples in the Bible would testify to this. Remember, the runner in a great race goes through great pain and struggle to prepare himself. That struggle makes victory that much sweeter and more fulfilling.

As you pursue God's wonderful plan for your life, remember that there would be no fulfillment in life without the struggle. Keep in mind—the greater the struggle, the greater the reward. Part of our reward is eternal and will come later. But here and now our reward is joy, true satisfaction, and real love. Those things that the world is trying to buy, acquire, or take pills to find, we have in Jesus through the Holy Spirit and our relationship with God.

Our path may not always be obvious. In fact, it is a narrow road, so partner with the Holy Spirit and journey toward your destiny. Consider this:

Enter through the narrow gate. For wide is the gate and broad is the road that leads to destruction, and many enter through it. But small is the gate and narrow the road that leads to life and only a few find it (Matthew 7:13-14).

ACTION & VISUALIZATION

When making a decision, pray that the Holy Spirit will guide you down the narrow road.

MEDITATION POINT

The Holy Spirit is your guide to a more intimate relationship with God—not the crowd.

Go to Chapter 4 in the Study Guide section on page 287.

ENDNOTES

1. Jack Hayford, ed., *Spirit Filled Life Bible for Students* (Nashville, TN: Thomas Nelson Publishers, 1995), 1370.

2. Ibid., 1260.

Chapter 5

Gift #2—The Holy Spirit (Part 2)

How do you make the Holy Spirit relevant in your life?

Before you begin reading, pray that the Holy Spirit
will give you understanding and application.

✝ [Jesus said] *"When the Counselor comes, Whom I will send to you
from the Father, the Spirit of truth who goes out from the Father, He
will testify about Me"* (John 15:26).

✝ [Jesus said] *"Therefore go and make disciples of all nations, baptizing
them in the name of the Father and of the Son and of the Holy Spirit,
and teaching them to obey everything I have commanded you. And
surely I am with you always, to the very end of the age"* (Matthew
28:19-20).

If you have ever done any public speaking, you probably had to overcome a certain amount of fear. "What if I blank out and forget what I was going to say? What if I freeze? What if I get people's names wrong? Is there spinach in my teeth?" It's nerve-racking to say the least. On a grand scale, we as believers are destined to fail, freeze, and blank out at times without the power of the Holy Spirit involved in our witnessing. Truth is, we need the help. We want to live with purpose and passion, we want our lives to stand for truth, we want to love and be loved, but how do we do all that? How do we find that power?

To feel some level of anxiety when you hear about your responsibility in the Great Commission (see Matthew 28:19-20) is normal—and in line with what Jesus expects. It is your calling as a Believer to make disciples and bring others to Christ. This may seem overwhelming (especially if you're still reeling from all of the stuff you're learning as a new Christian). But once again, you're not alone. The Holy Spirit testifies and gives witness to who Jesus is; He helps you relay this to your friends, your family...the whole world.

✞ [Jesus said] *"But you will receive power when the Holy Spirit comes on you; and you will be My witnesses in Jerusalem, and in all Judea and Samaria, and to the ends of the earth"* (Acts 1:8).

This is a very important aspect in becoming a mature Christian. You have become part of the Christian body, so it is important for you to be unified with a body of Believers who are passionate about bringing God's plan for salvation to the world. You will find true fulfillment in reflecting God's image and likeness with others—shining His light into the world together. This evidence of Him in us is our strongest testimony to the world. *Actions speak louder than words.*

So *you* have a *big* part to play in this plan.

Dedicated Christians are called disciples. Yes, when you dedicate yourself to Christ, you become one of His disciples—not unlike those who spent time with Him while he taught, preached, and healed during His earthly ministry. Disciples not only work at improving their own spirituality, but also reach out to others, encouraging, supporting, teaching, and training others in the things of God. In other words disciples are charged with duplicating themselves by helping create others who can be equipped to duplicate themselves, and so on.

Jesus lived and died never leaving a 300-mile radius. He left only 12 disciples to bring His message to the whole world, and now today there are approximately 2 billion Christians worldwide.[1] At some point you will want to see that you are impacting 12 others who are going out and doing the same so you can be an active part of the expansion of God's presence on earth. God asks us to be His hands, arms, legs, and mouth—to serve and witness to unbelievers as well as grow and help others (the Church) grow in Christ. Like Christ's disciples, you are *not only* to affect *your* generation, but also those yet to come.

God doesn't expect you to be a brilliant speaker or preacher or teacher. The first step to making a disciple is to simply be a witness to what Christ has done in your life. A witness is someone who tells what he or she has *experienced*. If you have accepted Christ as your Savior then you already have an *experience* to talk about. What's *your story*? How did Jesus find you? How did He draw you to Himself? How is He changing you? What is He doing for you?

When you share these things God has done or is doing in your life you will not only make a positive impact on others, you will also reinforce your own faith. So that anxiety you feel? It's a spiritual prompting to tell others what you have experienced. It is a God-planted desire to share what you know is a wonderful (and eternal) gift.

LET THE HOLY SPIRIT WORK

There are two things to remember about being a witness for Jesus. First—don't condemn others or start arguments. Instead, simply give your testimony, tell what you have *experienced* and let the Holy Spirit give them understanding as *only* He can. People may argue with your theories or theology, but they can't argue with *your story*. A person's salvation is usually a process that ends in a decision. The Bible says this process is like growing a plant, someone plants a seed, someone waters the plant—but only God makes it grow.

✝ *I [Paul] planted the seed, Apollos watered it, but God made it grow. So neither he who plants nor he who waters is anything, but only God, who makes things grow. The man who plants and the man who waters have one purpose, and each will be rewarded according to his own labor* (1 Corinthians 3:6-8).

You will not know ahead of time whether you are a "sower" or a "waterer" in the process. Pray for guidance from the Holy Spirit as you testify about your faith, then trust that He will do His part. The Holy Spirit will give you the words to say:

✝ *Whenever you are arrested and brought to trial, do not worry beforehand about what to say. Just say whatever is given you at the time, for it is not you speaking, but the Holy* Spirit (Mark 13:11).

You may be tempted to look for immediate results from the seeds you've planted or watered, but God's timing is not ours. We can become impatient, especially when we're reaching out to a loved one.

My wife was saved before I was, and her words weren't taking root in my heart. So much so that she and two of our children moved to Hawaii to live with my mom. However, she continued to water her words with prayer, which, I believe, led me to mysteriously stop at a church one Sunday during that period. Ultimately she was rewarded with an interesting phone call. She intended to tell me that she was going to be water baptized the next Sunday at Calvary Chapel in Honolulu. But before she could tell me her exciting news, I interrupted her with news of my own—I had arranged to be water baptized that same Sunday at Calvary Temple in Denver! Interesting coincidence? The Holy Spirit gives us the understanding to follow His perfect path at the perfect time.

Remember, it can take time for a seed to grow. Just look at nature—all plants blossom, bear fruit, and harvest according to their unique timetables. In the natural world you can't circumvent that process; however, you can cultivate the spiritual seed you've planted in someone by praying for them and relating to them in *God's love—love* is the key. Judgment, on the other hand, will *kill* anything you or others have planted. Here's a reminder of that kind of love:

Love is patient, love is kind. It does not envy, it does not boast, it is not proud. It is not rude, it is not self-seeking, it is not easily angered, it keeps no record of wrongs. Love does not delight in evil but rejoices with the truth. It always protects, always trusts, always hopes, always perseveres. Love never fails... (1 Corinthians 13:4-8).

Do you remember the story of the Samaritan woman in the Introduction? This is how the story continues:

Jesus said to her, "You are right when you say you have no husband. The fact is, you have had five husbands, and the man you now have is not your husband. What you have just said is quite true" (John 4:18).

Jesus told her something that went straight to the heart of her life and because of this she immediately believed in Him as the Savior.

✟ *Many of the Samaritans from that town believed in him because of the woman's testimony: "He told me everything I ever did"* (John 4:39).

The Samaritan woman felt Jesus touching her at the core of who she was. She knew from what He said that He knew her. He identified the empty part of her life that she had repeatedly tried to fill with men. She was excited because Jesus revealed that her emptiness could now be filled with Living Water—Jesus Himself. We all have multiple issues in our lives that, if touched, could make a dramatic impact on us.

Sometimes all we need to hear is one word. This was true for me. The word I needed to hear was *simplify*. Life had become complex for me because I had no absolute truth, no compass to guide me. Everything was a shade of gray. God simplified things for me by providing one truth—one truth with which to navigate my life. When I walked into church that Sunday morning, I was seeking an answer. I was primed to listen to God, therefore I heard Him. The Bible says that the seed (the Word of God) needs to fall on good soil to grow. That "good soil" is a heart that's open to hear God.

✟ *Still other seed fell on good soil. It came up, grew, and produced a crop, multiplying thirty, sixty, or even a hundred times* (Mark 4:8).

Sometimes the task we have as a disciple is *not* to plant, but to *till* the soil—to encourage people to ask questions. How do you till the soil? It's done through praying, loving, and caring as well as being there to lend a helping hand. Remember this saying: People don't care about what you know unless they know you care.

✠ [God says] *"Break up your unplowed* [hard] *ground* [heart] *and do not sow among thorns* [conflicting ideas]" (Jeremiah 4:3).

Indeed, people often ignore answers to questions they did *not* ask. In fact all of us have built-in defense mechanisms to justify what we do and to justify what we believe. Offering answers to someone who hasn't even asked a question will only trigger their defense mechanisms and likely create an argument—at this point you're trying to plant in the hard soil.

Instead, allow the Holy Spirit to guide you. After all, only He can lead us to a blind spot in a person's defense system or give us divine insight to simply offer our friendship, our service, or resources that will till the ground and position us for the right timing, making them receptive to future seeds.

It is critical to trust and listen to the Holy Spirit when we testify to others. It may be tempting to speak to a specific issue we know a friend or family member has. We might think this is the issue where God can reach them best, but it may *not* be as obvious as you think. Be cautious and make sure your anxiety doesn't turn to desperation which will override wisdom.

A desperate attitude can be counterproductive. As a salesman, I know through experience that if you need a sale badly, projecting this attitude can negatively impact the ability to "close the deal." Just do your part—share what you believe the Holy Spirit wants you to share—then let Him *complete* the work you started.

As the Holy Spirit gives you spiritual witness to Christ, make sure your physical witness does the same. In other words, is your lifestyle reflecting Christ? If people can see changes in your life, your actions will testify in ways words cannot. Mahatma Gandhi noted, "I like your Christ, I do not like your Christians. Your Christians are so unlike your Christ."[2] If you want to make a real impact on the people you care about, then start growing yourself into His image and likeness. It will be hard to deny His presence and power when others *see* and *feel* it flowing *out* of you.

ACTION & VISUALIZATION

Be a witness of Jesus Christ whenever possible. Pray for the Holy Spirit to give you the words to say and the actions to do as well as to give them the ears to hear and the sight to see.

BOLDNESS

Perhaps you're still feeling a bit uncertain about testifying. Are you concerned you will fumble with your words? Or maybe you're fearful or shy around those who don't know about your salvation. Do you have family members who are hostile toward believers? If so, you are feeling what many of the early Christians felt. Like them, step out in *faith* to witness under the prompting of the Holy Spirit, and the Holy Spirit will give you *boldness*.

✠ *After they prayed, the place where they were meeting was shaken. And they were all **filled** with the Holy Spirit and spoke the word of God **boldly** (Acts 4:31).*

The word for boldness used here, *parrhesia* (par-rhay-see-ah), means "outspokenness" or "freedom of speech, with frankness, candor, cheerfulness, and courage." It's the opposite of cowardice, timidity, or fear. In this context it denotes a divine enablement giving ordinary people spiritual authority and power. It also refers to a clear and understandable presentation of the Gospel. *Parrhesia* is not a human quality but the result of following the leading of the Holy Spirit. It is not emotional hype, hysteria, or fanaticism. It is a *confidence* produced by the Holy Spirit that moves through a person, allowing that person to act as a conduit for divine power and ability.[3]

You will feel this yourself when you step up and follow the leading of the Holy Spirit. And He *will* lead you:

While Peter was still thinking about the vision, the Spirit said to him, "Simon, three men are looking for you. So get up and go downstairs. Do not hesitate to go with them, for I have sent them" (Acts 10:19-20).

POWER

The Holy Spirit enhances our abilities. The "heroes" of the Bible were regular people just like you and me; however, the Holy Spirit came upon them and allowed them to do great things. Read what the Bible says about some of these men:

Then the Spirit of the Lord came upon Gideon…(Judges 6:34).

The Spirit of the Lord came upon him [Samson] *in power so that he tore the lion apart with his bare hands as he might have torn a young goat. But he told neither his father nor his mother what he had done* (Judges 14:6).

As he [Samson] *approached Lehi, the Philistines came toward him shouting. The Spirit of the Lord came upon him in power. The ropes on his arms became like charred flax, and the bindings dropped from his hands* (Judges 15:14).

✠ *Then the Lord said, "Rise and anoint him* [David]; *he is the one." So Samuel took the horn of oil and anointed him* [David] *in the presence of his brothers, and from that day on the Spirit of the Lord came upon David in power...* (1 Samuel 16:12-13).

✠ *The power of the Lord came upon Elijah and, tucking his cloak into his belt, he ran ahead of Ahab* [who was on a chariot] *all the way to Jezreel* (1 Kings 18:46).

Now I am not suggesting you will suddenly have the ability to slay lions, defeat thousands, and heal people like these men of the Bible. But I *am* saying that as you grow spiritually and start learning to work with the Holy Spirit, you can experience spiritual power in your life *beyond* your natural power, intellect, and abilities. The possibilities are limitless even if they are unimaginable to you right now.

HOPE AND MORE

I'm sure you're starting to get the picture that the Holy Spirit plays a huge role in our lives as Christians. And there's still more! The Holy Spirit gives us hope:

✠ *May the God of hope fill you with all joy and peace as you trust in Him, so that you may overflow with hope by the power of the Holy Spirit* (Romans 15:13).

It is hope that allows us to experience joy and peace even as we go through trials, challenges, or battles in life. The Holy Spirit knows the future, so He can tell you things yet to come that you can use to build up your hope.

✝ [Jesus said] *"But when He, the Spirit of truth, comes, He will guide you into all truth. He will not speak on His own; He will speak only what He hears, and He will tell you what is yet to come"* (John 16:13).

The Holy Spirit is the conduit for prophecy:

✝ *For prophecy never had its origin in the will of man, but men spoke from God as they were carried along by the Holy Spirit* (2 Peter 1:21).

The Holy Spirit prays God's will for us:

✝ *In the same way, the Spirit helps us in our weakness. We do not know what we ought to pray for, but the Spirit Himself intercedes for us with groans that words cannot express. And He who searches our hearts knows the mind of the Spirit, because the Spirit intercedes for the saints in accordance with God's will* (Romans 8:26-27).

And it is the Holy Spirit who gives us favor with others:

✝ *The king had granted him* [Ezra] *everything he asked, for the Hand of the Lord* [Holy Spirit] *his God was on him* (Ezra 7:6).

A restored connection to God through the Holy Spirit brings you access to God's guidance, power, and knowledge. It's important to note, though, you still have a free choice—you can pursue or ignore this new life-enhancing relationship. Choosing to listen to the Holy Spirit will give you access to all the things He can provide you, including power, love, hope, confidence, joy, peace, and more.

SUBJECTING YOUR WILL

God's guidance, power, and knowledge are not the only benefits of a connection with Him. Some other benefits are known as fruits of the Spirit. The fruits of the Spirit can flow into you and out onto other people's lives in large measure. What are these fruits? They are the attributes and the nature of God that were intended for us in His original design for us. The Bible describes these fruits of the Spirit as follows:

✟ *But the fruit of the Spirit is love, joy, peace, patience, kindness, good-ness, faithfulness, gentleness and self-control...* (Galatians 5:22-23).

We consume these attributes from the Holy Spirit so we can give them away to *all* those around us. When we can live out these attributes in our lives now and help others see Jesus—we become fruit-bearers. Imagine if everyone in the world was bearing fruit. That's the world God intended for us to live in and benefit from—a world where everyone we meet shows us love. Read what Jesus said about bearing fruit:

✟ *This is to My Father's glory, that you bear much fruit, **showing your-selves to be My disciples*** (John 15:8).

You have read that at our spiritual birth we are given a new heart. With this new heart and God's Spirit in you, God expects this newly empowered you to choose to bear much fruit. You will have opportunities in everyday life to choose to bear fruit. Jesus told His disciples a parable:

✚ *A man had a fig tree, planted in his vineyard, and he went to look for fruit on it, but did not find any. So he said to the man who took care of the vineyard, "For three years now I've been coming to look for fruit on this fig tree and haven't found any. Cut it down! Why should it use up the soil?" "Sir," the man replied, "leave it alone for one more year, and I'll dig around it and fertilize it. If it bears fruit next year, fine! If not, then cut it down"* (Luke 13:6-9).

God expects us to bear fruit, but He gives us time to do it. God also offers us His help to accomplish our fruit-bearing mission. Jesus describes it this way:

✚ *I am the true Vine, and my Father is the gardener. He cuts off every branch in Me that bears no fruit, while every branch that does bear fruit He prunes so that it will be even more fruitful. You are already clean because of the word I have spoken to you. Remain in Me, and I will remain in you. No branch can bear fruit by itself; it must remain in the vine. Neither can you bear fruit unless you remain in Me. I am the Vine; you are the branches. If a man remains in Me and I in him, he will bear much fruit; apart from Me you can do nothing"* (John 15:1-5).

The pruning can be painful, yet it is an important process that allows the Holy Spirit to flow freely in all aspects of our lives. Your focus on bearing fruit will become important to you. I can tell you from experience that pruning can be painful, but like the pruning of plants, it's always beneficial. When you bear much fruit, you will benefit because you will receive much fruit—what you sow, you will reap in due time. Did you notice from this passage that you can't produce the fruit alone? (He is the vine and we are the fruit that grows off of it.) This concept of God being the source of the good things we produce is found throughout the Bible.

☦ *If anyone does not remain in Me, he is like a branch that is thrown away and withers; such branches are picked up, thrown into the fire and burned* (John 15:6).

This is a good reason to be actively working together with God to bear fruit because you are merely a conduit through which God's attributes will flow. To do this, you must seek God's will above your own—you must subject your will to His. How do you do this? Start with prayer. Ask God to *show* you His will. Then *listen* to the Holy Spirit who will help you recognize God's will and complete the work by giving you *strength* and the ability to follow through on His prompting.

Being in sync with God's will allows you to fire up His power much like the distributor in a car. If the spark plugs don't fire in sync with the release of fuel into the piston chamber, the car won't start. When you consider God's will and count on the Holy Spirit to help with your decision making, you'll discover something that will guide you in all aspects of life—*wisdom*.

☦ *...And the breath of the Almighty* [Holy Spirit] *gives him* [man] *understanding. Great men are not always wise...*(Job 32:8-9 NKJV).

☦ *To the man who pleases Him, God gives wisdom, knowledge and happiness...* (Ecclesiastes 2:26).

Wisdom is much better than knowledge. Knowledge is simply possessing information, but wisdom leads you to the correct use of that information. Wisdom for Christians means taking knowledge and applying God's guidelines and truths to it.

✝ *My* [wisdom's] *fruit is better than fine gold...*(Proverbs 8:19).

✝ *Wisdom makes one wise man more powerful than ten rulers in a city* (Ecclesiastes 7:19).

✝ *A prudent* [wise] *man sees danger and takes refuge, but the simple keep going and suffer for it* (Proverbs 22:3).

✝ *Blessed is the man who finds wisdom, the man who gains understanding, for she* [wisdom] *is more profitable than silver and yields better returns than gold. She is more precious than rubies; nothing you desire can compare with her. Long life is in her right hand; in her left hand are riches and honor. Her ways are pleasant ways, and all her paths are peace. She is a tree of life to those who embrace her; those who lay hold of her will be blessed* (Proverbs 3:13-18).

When faced with a choice, I recommend you always ask yourself the defining question: "What is the *wise* thing to do?"

Baptism in the Spirit

We choose to be baptized into Jesus death and resurrection. Baptism in the Holy Spirit is done in much the same way—it is a choice. This second baptism, like the first, is a stepping stone on our journey toward the image and likeness of Christ:

✠ *Therefore let us leave the elementary teachings about Christ and go on to maturity, not laying again the foundation of repentance from acts that lead to death, and of faith in God, instruction about baptisms...* (Hebrews 6:1-2).

You will note the "s" on the word baptism, which suggests more than one. Actually, there are two baptisms in your Christian walk. You see this recorded in several instances in the Bible where people who have already been water baptized are encouraged to be baptized in the Holy Spirit.

✠ *When the apostles in Jerusalem heard that Samaria had accepted the word of God, they sent Peter and John to them. When they arrived, they prayed for them that they might receive the Holy Spirit, because the Holy Spirit had not yet come upon any of them; they had simply been baptized into the name of the Lord Jesus* [which means they did have the Holy Spirit *in* them *already*]. *Then Peter and John placed their hands on them, and they received the Holy Spirit* [sometimes referred to as *on* them when speaking about the Holy Spirit baptism] (Acts 8:14-17).

I like to think of our developing relationship with God as a three-step process: accepting Christ; water baptism; and Holy Spirit baptism. The first step is to simply accept Christ as your personal Savior. This is what reconnects God's Spirit within you and provides you with the promise of eternal life. The second step is to identify with and commit yourself to Jesus by being baptized in water. This is important to symbolize and memorialize your relationship with Jesus, His death, and resurrection. Think of it as a wedding ceremony that publicly announces the commitment between husband and wife. And step three is being baptized in the Holy Spirit.

Holy Spirit baptism is when you memorialize your relationship with the Holy Spirit. While the details or process may vary from one church to the next, typically an elder of the Body of Christ will lay hands on you and ask the Holy Spirit to be present and active in guiding you through life. Or in a time of spiritual closeness you may simply ask the Holy Spirit yourself to come into your life and guide you. I believe baptism in the Holy Spirit is your action of faith to Him the Holy Spirit, a way to express your intent and desire to follow His prompting not just initially, but *daily*. Some believers put too much emphasis on the ceremonial aspect of the Baptism in the Holy Spirit versus its intended daily application of actually following Him. Following His daily lead allows the Holy Spirit to do things through you beyond your natural talents, intellect, and abilities. Indeed many believers who have not specifically opted to go through the ceremonial Baptism of the Holy Spirit still lead supernatural lives by following His lead daily.

THE ROOTS OF THE STORY

I believe this three-step progression of faith was foretold in the Old Testament Book of Exodus. In fact, this Old Testament story which outlines this three step progress of faith is prominent in understanding the Gifts of Freedom. Let's explore this story together.

First a little background. In the Old Testament Book of Genesis, we learn that God promised Abraham he would have many descendants. He also promised these descendants (referred to as Israelites) would inherit a rich and fertile land—the Promised Land.

The Lord had said to Abram [Abraham] *"Leave your country, your people and your father's household and go to the land I will show you. I will make you into a great nation and I will bless you; I will make your name great, and you will be a blessing"* (Genesis 12:1-2).

Skip ahead a few years—the Israelites have been taken into captivity in Egypt and forced to live as slaves under the harsh rule of the Pharaoh; however, they still had this promise from God.

⊕ *And I have promised to bring you up out of your misery into the land* [Promised Land]... *a land flowing with milk and honey* (Exodus 3:17).

God then raises up Moses (an Israelite) from within Pharaoh's household and charges him with setting the Israelites free to bring them back to this Promised Land. One of the ways God does this is by granting Moses the power to perform dramatic miracles intended to convince the Pharaoh to let the people go free. (Perhaps you recall the ten plagues on Egypt? See Exodus 7-11.) These miracles get the Pharaoh's attention, but it's only the last one—a plague intended to kill all firstborn sons—that convinces Pharaoh to let the Israelites leave his kingdom. It's important to note how God protected the Israelites' sons from this plague. God instructed them to sacrifice an unblemished (innocent) lamb and apply the blood from that lamb to the doorpost and lintel of their homes.

⊕ *When the Lord goes through the land to strike down the Egyptians, He will see the blood* [of the innocent lamb] *on the top and sides of the doorframe and will pass over that doorway, and He will not permit the destroyer* [death] *to enter your houses and strike you down. Obey these instructions as a lasting ordinance for you and your descendants. When you enter the land that the Lord will give you as He promised, observe this* [Passover] *ceremony* (Exodus 12:23-25).

You are probably familiar with the next part of the story. When the Pharaoh's firstborn son dies, he finally relents and lets the Israelites go. Moses leads the Israelites out of Egypt. They didn't get far before Pharaoh had a change of heart and started chasing after them. Backed up against the Red Sea, God gave Moses the power to part the sea and let the Israelites cross, narrowly escaping the Egyptian armies. Then the sea destroyed the pursuing army which was seeking to take them back into captivity.

✠ *Moses stretched out his hand over the sea, and at daybreak the sea went back to its place. The Egyptians were fleeing toward it, and the Lord swept them into the sea. The water flowed back and covered the chariots and horsemen—the entire army of Pharaoh that had followed the Israelites into the sea. Not one of them survived* (Exodus 14:27-28).

After such a miraculous feat, you would think the Israelites would have been ready to trust God with anything. But as Moses led them to the Jordan River, near the Promised Land, this turned out to be false. Moses sent 12 spies to scout out the land. Ten of the spies returned with reports of unbeatable foes—they even called them "giants"—and the Israelites were *frightened* by those reports. Because they weren't ready to trust God when facing the new enemies, they wandered in the wilderness for *40 years* before their children were permitted to enter the Promised Land.

There's more to this story, but let's step back for a moment to see how the overall story up to this point applies to the Gifts of Freedom. Before we accept the gift of salvation, you and I—and all people—are like the enslaved Israelites. We escape the angel of death not by the blood of an innocent lamb on our doorpost, but by the blood of Jesus on the post of the Cross.

✠ *...For Christ, our Passover Lamb, has been sacrificed* (1 Corinthians 5:7).

We're captives, not to Pharaoh, but to sin. Just as God sent Moses to save the people from their slavery, He sent Jesus to save us and set us free from the bondage of sin. Like the Israelites, we are set free. But to live in that freedom, we have to follow Jesus, just as the Israelites had to follow Moses out of their slavery in Egypt. It's interesting that the first miracle Moses performed for Pharaoh was turning the waters of Egypt to blood. Likewise, the first recorded miracle Jesus performed was turning water into wine (a symbol of blood) at a wedding ceremony. (See John 2:1-11.)

The Red Sea crossing represents our water baptism. Though we are set free by Jesus, we are called to identify with Him through baptism. Just as the Israelites went into the "water" and then came up out of it on the other side freed from their captives who were buried in the water, we do the same when we are baptized. As noted in an earlier chapter, this baptism is a way of identifying with Jesus' death (shedding of His blood) and resurrection. I believe it is no coincidence that the sea is called the Red Sea.

Now what about the Promised Land? For the Israelites, this was a land they would call their own—a home and place where they could become the nation God intended for them. For you and me, the Promised Land is the place where we can become the people God intended us to be—a home where we can conform to the *image and likeness of God*. Remember, we are spirit beings and there are areas we must conquer in this life to more fully inhabit our Promised Land—*our minds and bodies*.

The Israelites didn't cross the Jordan River the first time they encountered it. God had promised them the land! Shouldn't it have been a forgone conclusion that God would supernaturally give them victory against any occupants in the land—even "giants?" You would think so, but they didn't have enough faith.

✝ *So we see that they were not able to enter, because of their unbelief* (Hebrews 3:19).

They were afraid to go into the land because they didn't think they could defeat the inhabitants even with God's promise to help. Many believers don't have the faith it takes to seek entry into their Promised Land (image and likeness of God) because they don't believe they can be successful at subdueing the enemy in their mind and body. Perhaps you're a little fearful about what it will take to conform to the image and likeness of Christ. But fear not, you have a promise from God to help you. The first step for the Israelites to achieve the occupation of the Promised Land was to cross the Jordan River. For you and me, I believe this river crossing represents the baptism of the Holy Spirit or our commitment to following the leading of the Holy Spirit in our daily lives. It's an act of faith to trust God to lead us to victory so we can safely inhabit our Promised Land.

Looking at this Old Testament account spiritually, we see God's promise to bring us back into His image and likeness (into the Promised Land). However, the degree to which you have faith in the Holy Spirit—to ascertain God's will for your life and then rely on Him to help you regain possession of your Promised Land—is the degree to which you can start taking possession of that land.

Ten spies didn't have that faith, but two did. Two spies knew that it was possible.

✠ *Then Caleb* [one of the two faith filled spies] *silenced the people before Moses and said "we should go up and take possession of the land, **for we can certainly do it**"* (Numbers 13:30).

Caleb's faith in God was speaking. But it wasn't enough to convince the Israelites and they continued to wander through the wilderness. This is where many Christians are—wandering through life, just getting by, and not entering their God-promised Promised Land.

It's important to note that despite their undeveloped faith, they weren't wandering alone—God was still with them. He even provided them with food when they needed it, raining food (manna) from the heavens. I think this was God's way of training the Israelites' faith by showing them He was their daily provider. And so it is for some of us—we accept Christ and get baptized in Christ, and then find ourselves wandering around in the wilderness. However, we're called to seek guidance, strength and joy from the Holy Spirit, not letting worldly ups and downs affect our ability to become all that God wants us to be. And still, all this time, God is giving us our daily provision.

ENTERING THE PROMISED LAND

When the Israelites finally did cross the Jordan to enter the Promised Land, they did so by letting go of their fears and trusting God's leading. Life didn't suddenly become perfect and pain-free—they would face many battles to possess the land—but they trusted God's power to help them overcome obstacles. This is the way for us, too. When we are baptized in the Spirit, we need to let go of the fears produced by our natural mind and instead trust the Holy Spirit's leading and power.

The story of the Israelites' first major battle in the Promised Land is a great illustration of this trust. Jericho was a well-fortified city—a stronghold surrounded by high walls. God told the Israelites to march around the city for six days in a row, and then to march around the city seven more times on the seventh day, blowing their horns and shouting. Does this seem like sound military strategy to you? No, at least not to your natural mind. But they did this anyway *in faith* and *obedience* to God, and the walls crumbled to the ground. (See Joshua 6:1-20.)

In a spiritual sense, we face strongholds in our lives, too. What are strongholds? Spiritually speaking, strongholds are the thoughts and habits that are contrary to God's will—Godless thinking we build up over time with our natural minds and physical desires. They keep us from fully occupying our Promised Land, and from conforming to the *image and likeness of God*. When we trust the Holy Spirit's guidance, we can defeat these strongholds in our lives and bring them down.

The most critical step in any endeavor is to find God's will. Ask yourself this question: Am I in sync with God's will for my life?

The Holy Spirit is always available to help you get in sync with God's will. He reveals where you need to be and what you need to do to bring down the strongholds holding you back. Don't be surprised when the Holy Spirit leads you to do the unexpected. It's His style! The Israelites could not bring down Jericho with their own efforts, weapons, or intellect, but once they accepted the fact that God knew what He was doing (and obeyed Him), they received victory. God can do unbelievable things in our lives, both physically and spiritually, if we obediently work with Him and His representative in us, the Holy Spirit.

So you see it is not simply crossing the Jordan (receiving the baptism of the Holy Spirit) that allows you to fully possess the Promised Land. To actually occupy it you must take the territory that is inhabited by enemy strongholds—thoughts and habits not aligned with God's will. God will supply the knowledge and power to take them down *if* you continually seek His will and trust the Holy Spirit to lead you.

Here's one more thought on this subject that helps to tie the Old Testament and New Testament stories together as it relates to baptism of the Holy Spirit. Just prior to starting His ministry, Jesus was water baptized. It is at this water baptism when He is simultaneously baptized in the Spirit as was the case much of the time in the early New Testament church.

✝ *Then Jesus came from Galilee to the Jordan to be baptized by John* [the Baptist]. *...As soon as Jesus was baptized, He went up out of the* *water. At that moment Heaven was opened, and He saw the Spirit of God descending like a dove and lighting on Him* (Matthew 3:13,16).

This is the very same Jordan River you just read about that represented the baptism of the Spirit for the Israelites 1,400 years earlier. Amazing, don't you think? God's story is an intricate weaving designed to send us a clear message.

Would you like to seek this intimate relationship with the Holy Spirit and give Him your allegiance?

ACTION & VISUALIZATION

Arrange with a pastor or church elder for prayer to receive the baptism of the Holy Spirit, or simply pray yourself.

EFFECTS OF THE BAPTISM OF THE SPIRIT

What does it look like to be baptized in the Spirit? We get a glimpse of this in the Book of Acts—where the Holy Spirit comes upon the disciples for the first time.

✝ *When the day of Pentecost came, they were all together in one place. Suddenly a sound like the blowing of a violent wind came from Heaven and filled the whole house where they were sitting. They saw what seemed to be tongues of fire that separated and came to rest on each of them. All of them were filled with the Holy Spirit and began to speak in other tongues as the Spirit enabled them* (Acts 2:1-4).

When you are baptized in the *Holy Spirit* you probably won't experience this dramatic of a Pentecost experience due to the spiritual season we are in. However, it is not unusual to have a manifestation of the *gift* of tongues and/or other specific gifts residing in you. I will speak more about these other Gifts of the Spirit in Book Three, but I'd like to talk a bit about the gift of tongues now—which is a heavenly language many receive at their baptism of the Spirit.

✟ *While Peter was still speaking these words, the Holy Spirit came on all who heard the message. The circumcised believers who had come with Peter were astonished that the gift of the Holy Spirit had been poured out even on the Gentiles. For they heard them speaking in tongues and praising God. Then Peter said, "Can anyone keep these people from being baptized with water? They have received the Holy Spirit just as we have"* (Acts 10:44-47).

When you accept the gift of salvation, the Holy Spirit enters into you and begins speaking with you in a language your natural mind can understand. But the gift of tongues is something different—it is a language God understands and your spirit understands, however, your natural mind does not. The Holy Spirit gives these utterances—we don't choose the words, but we do have to choose to let these utterances flow from us.

✟ *This is what they speak* [tongues], *not in words taught to us by human wisdom but in words taught by the Spirit, expressing spiritual truths in spiritual words* (1 Corinthians 2:13).

The gift of tongues is something that will flow out when the Holy Spirit comes upon you. While I may have received the language from God when I was baptized in the Holy Spirit, I did not actually let it start flowing until a short time later. Initially it came from my spirit when I fell into deeper worship and concentration on God.

This heavenly language was prophesied about in the Old Testament:

✟ *For then I will restore to the peoples a pure language, that they may all call on the name of the Lord, to serve Him with one accord* (Zephaniah 3:9 NKJV).

And then the Apostle Paul said:

✟ *For anyone who speaks in a tongue does not speak to men but to God. Indeed, no one understands him; he utters mysteries with his spirit* (1 Corinthians 14:2).

ACTION & VISUALIZATION

Pray that you may receive your heavenly language
and learn to flow with the Spirit's outpouring of that language.

The Holy Spirit can lead you to use this language in prayer when you don't know what to pray for. This keeps your natural mind out of the way and allows the Holy Spirit to pray in agreement with God's will because the Holy Spirit knows what to pray for:

✟ *In the same way, the Spirit helps us in our weakness. We do not know what we ought to pray for, but the Spirit Himself intercedes for us with groans that words cannot express* (Romans 8:26).

✠ *For if I pray in a tongue, my spirit prays, but my mind is unfruitful. So what shall I do? I will pray with my spirit, but I will also pray with my mind; I will sing with my spirit, but I will also sing with my mind* (1 Corinthians 14:14-15).

✠ *But you, dear friends, build yourselves up in your most holy faith and pray in the Holy Spirit* (Jude 1:20).

It is good when the Holy Spirit leads us to pray and sing to God in tongues. Indeed, this is a way for you to allow God's will to be prayed into your life without the interference of your will.

As this chapter comes to a close, I'd like to turn your attention to something Jesus teaches and that helps us understand more about the Holy Spirit. This lesson is recorded in two of the Gospels, but there is a subtle difference between them that speaks volumes. In the Gospel of Luke, Jesus says:

✠ *So I say to you: Ask and it will be given to you; seek and you will find; knock and the door will be opened to you. For everyone who asks receives; he who seeks finds; and to him who knocks, the door will be opened. Which of you fathers, if your son asks for a fish, will give him a snake instead? Or if he asks for an egg, will give him a scorpion? If you then, though you are evil, know how to give good gifts to your children, how much more will your Father in Heaven give the* **Holy Spirit** *to those who ask Him!* (Luke 11:9-13)

The lesson is repeated in the Gospel of Matthew almost verbatim except in the last sentence the Holy Spirit's name is replaced with the name of what He means to us:

✝ *How much more will your Father in Heaven give **good gifts** to those who ask Him!* (Matthew 7:11)

I believe it is clear: the *Holy Spirit* is our source for all *good gifts.*

✝ *...where the Spirit of the Lord is, there is **freedom*** (2 Corinthians 3:17).

The Holy Spirit is a really *big* gift—He assists us in receiving and using the rest of the Gifts of Freedom. Partnership with the Holy Spirit is essential. It leads you to receiving all God's gifts so you can gain the *freedom* to fully occupy the land God desires especially for you.

MEDITATION POINT

The Holy Spirit will deliver to you the Gifts of Freedom that if you wear them they will prepare you for an intimate relationship with God Himself.

Go to Chapter 5 in the Study Guide section on page 293.

ENDNOTES

1. About.com. "Denominations." Retrieved April 5, 2008, from http://christianity.about.com/od/denominations/p/christiantoday.htm.

2. Brainyquote.com. "Quotes." Retrieved April 5, 2008, from http://www.brainyquote.com/quotes/quotes/m/mohandasga107529. html.

3. Jack Hayford, ed., *Spirit Filled Life Bible for Students* (Nashville, TN: Thomas Nelson Publishers, 1995), 1392.

CHAPTER 6

GIFT #3—FAITH (PART 1)

WHY IS FAITH NEEDED TO UNITE GOD'S GIFTS?

Before you begin to read, pray that the Holy Spirit
will give you understanding and application.

✝ *...think soberly, as God has dealt to each one a measure of faith*
(Romans 12:3 NKJV).

C an you truly capture the immensity of the Grand Canyon based on a postcard picture? Can the grandeur of Niagara Falls truly be described with words alone? How about your favorite beach—do your vacation pictures really do it justice? If you've been to these or other amazing places, you may have snapshots you can show your friends, but two-dimensional images pale in comparison to the first-hand experience. "You have to check this out for yourself!" you might say as you show them the pictures.

Honestly, this book as well as all Christian books and even the Bible can only go so far in presenting what faith is all about. Words, pictures, and instructions are only snapshots—if you want the real thing, you'll have to receive, unwrap, and use faith for yourself. Indeed, unless you do, the Bible and God's words to you will be little more than words.

✟ *For we also have had the gospel preached to us,...**but** the message
they heard was of **no** value to them, because those who heard did not
combine it with **faith** (Hebrews 4:2).*

While the Spirit gives you *access* to all the other Gifts of Freedom, your
faith is the catalyst to bring them *alive*. It was faith that brought to life or
allowed you to unwrap the first two gifts—life and the Holy Spirit.

The Holy Spirit allows you to have understanding of the Message; however, you still need to use your faith for the Messages to become real to you
and have an impact on your life. The Holy Spirit delivers you the gifts, and
your faith helps you unwrap and use them.

So what is faith?

✟ *Now **faith** is being sure of what we hope for and certain of what we
do not see (Hebrews 11:1).*

That's an interesting phrase, "certain of what we do *not* see." This could
be a definition of trust, too. It's *not* easy to be certain of what you don't see,
especially when what you *see* sometimes is the opposite of what you were
hoping for. In fact, we couldn't be certain of anything we don't see—
whether spiritual or worldly—without God's gift of faith.

What about these "things we do not see." When used in the spiritual
context, this phrase applies to two different aspects of our lives. The first is
the Kingdom of God, a place where God Himself lives: this includes the
Spirit realm where invisible truths shape and influence our relationship
with Him. Obviously, we can not see Him or His truths with our eyes, so
we must have faith in them.

The second aspect is our physical realm—the place where we live and
breathe on this earth. There are things we have faith in God for in the

physical realm that haven't been manifested. Maybe you'd like to have many kids; you have been going through financial difficulty, yet believe by faith that God will provide. Remember being sure of what we hope for doesn't necessarily mean getting the exact results or the ideal timeframe we were expecting. God works in such complex ways beyond our understanding that many times it seems mysterious. In these instances, we must also have faith in Him and His intentions—that in the end He will work out everything for our ultimate good.

✠ *And we know that in **all things** God works for the **good** of those who love Him, who have been called according to His purpose (Romans 8:28).*

Keep in mind even outside your relationship with God, you currently act in faith everyday. You get up and go to work because you have faith that a paycheck you can't currently see will show up at the end of the week or month. You plant seeds in anticipation that they will grow. Whether you realize it or not you're using your faith mechanism every time you do anything based on the expectations of producing a specific result. Your actions based on God's Word and your love for Him please Him. The more you have to act without seeing the result you expect, the more you are *exercising* your faith. It takes stronger, better-developed faith to continue to act longer or more in faith before seeing a result. The more we exercise this idea of *acting in faith*, the *stronger* our faith gets in that area.

How important is faith in our relationship with God?

✠ *And without faith it is **impossible** to please God because anyone who comes to Him must believe that He exists and that He rewards those who earnestly seek Him (Hebrews 11:6).*

Faith is paramount to God. It breathes life into your relationship and all the other Gifts, helping you conform to His image and likeness. When you act in faith, you please God because your actions of faith reflect your trust and surrender to Him. *Faith is the key to His heart.* It takes faith to unwrap all the other gifts because they are spiritual in nature, not readily identifiable by our senses or mind. Therefore faith is required to act on them and to even make them real to us. The manifestation of the gift inside that you unwrap with your faith becomes your *reward* for your *action* of faith in unwrapping it.

On the surface, the verse in Romans (...*think soberly, as God has dealt to each one a measure of faith)* and the verse in Hebrews (*And without faith it is impossible to please God...*) seem to create an interesting conflict. Romans 12:3 clearly states that God determines the amount of faith each of us is to receive. Hebrews 11:6 seems to say it takes faith to please Him. If God determines the amount of faith we each have, then doesn't that mean He alone determines or programs within us how much we can please Him? Sounds like a Catch 22, right? Thankfully, it's not. It is the *exhibition* or *use* of your faith that pleases God–*faith is action.* It doesn't matter how much faith we are given, it only matters if we *act* on it.

✝ ...*faith by itself, if it is not accompanied by action, is dead* (James 2:17).

God gives us the inanimate ability to have faith; however, it is up to us to *animate* that faith by *acting* on it. God gives us faith as a noun and we give it back to Him as a verb to please Him. While you can't "work" for more faith through your deeds (remember it is a gift); you can and are expected to *express* what you were given. It is acting in faith on *His* words that makes faith pleasing to God and at the same time allows you to grow, increase, and strengthen your faith.

Remember it was by faith and *only* faith that you were saved so that you could have right-standing with God:

✟ *For it is by grace you have been saved, through faith...* (Ephesians 2:8).

✟ *...to the man who does not work* [trust in their own good works] *but trusts God who justifies the wicked, his faith is credited as righteousness* (Romans 4:5).

Think about it. Faith has been given to you by God; however, you were not automatically saved by that faith. No, you had to *use* it. As it says in Romans 10:9, you had to exhibit an *action* of faith by *confessing* with your mouth and *believing* in your heart that Jesus is your Lord and Savior.

This is what many Christians call "saving faith." The word *saving* suggests the action that was taken as a result of a decision that you made to be saved. But your exhibition of saving faith was only the *initial* step that began your journey. This journey calls us to exhibit *daily* what I call a *living faith*.

✟ *...but the righteous will live by his faith* (Habakkuk 2:4).

As you do you'll begin to see an interesting phenomenon—when you accept and use a gift God offers you, you are in turn giving a gift back to God—the gift of fulfilling His will for your life.

Using Your Faith

Imagine staring at a snapshot of the Grand Canyon taken by a friend and wanting to see and experience it for yourself. Simply hoping or wanting to see the Grand Canyon doesn't make it happen. Doing this requires action. We must pack the car, fill it with gas, check the tires and the engine, get directions to the Grand Canyon, then drive. Doing all of this careful preparation in *faith* and *hope* that you'll experience what you saw in the snapshot doesn't ensure an easy, event-free trip. You still might run into bad weather or heavy traffic. And yet, your faith moves you forward to your goal, despite obstacles. What if you are in an accident along the way and end up in the hospital? You can give up hope of experiencing the Grand Canyon, or you can, in faith, *resume* your journey when you're released.

It's important to remember that we live in a fallen world brought about by our rejection of God. Therefore we are going to face obstacles along this journey of life.

✠ [God said after the fall] *"Cursed is the ground because of you; through painful toil you will eat of it all the days of your life"* (Genesis 3:17).

This is why it's going to be a struggle sometimes to have our hope manifest before we give up. But just as it takes persistence to make that journey to the Grand Canyon, it is our *persistent actions of faith* that allow us to fully experience what we hope in God for as well as the gifts God *offers* us. To *fully* experience the gifts He offers, we must continue with our actions of faith to unwrap them until we get the results He promises. Indeed the Hebrew word for *faith* indicates persistence.

GROWING YOUR FAITH

Because our lives are not suddenly perfect and trouble free when we accept the gift of life—we now have plenty of opportunities to live by faith. All living things grow and develop—even spiritual things. The way we grow our faith is similar to the way we grow our muscles—through exercise. If everything you ever wanted in life was brought to you on a silver platter and you didn't have to move physically to reach anything, eventually the muscles in your legs and arms would grow weaker and weaker until your sedentary lifestyle made it more difficult to run or even walk. The same is true of our faith.

What causes us to exercise our faith?

- When there is something we hope for, but we can't see it yet.

- When we continue to believe God will fulfill His promises.

- When we rely on God to provide for us, answer our prayers, and show up in challenging circumstances.

- When we wait for and act in anticipation of God's physical manifestation of what we hope for.

- When in any circumstance we base our actions on God's nature and good intentions for us—even when we don't understand the reason for what's happening.

Exercising your faith in all these situations will be the key to achieving new freedoms by the unwrapping and use of additional gifts.

✝ *For we walk by faith, not by sight* (2 Corinthians 5:7 NKJV).

Again, we live in a fallen world full of fallen people doing things *not* in the will of God, so we'll encounter *many* things we don't expect to see—things we don't understand—and many of them will be painful or difficult physically, relationally, or circumstantially. Some of the things we'll encounter are the result of man's fall which allowed evil into the world, or because we ignore spiritual laws, or because of our sin, or sometimes even evidence of God's discipline in our lives, or simply an attack by satan.

Understand that regardless of the cause, the trials and sufferings we encounter in life, despite the pain, are actually the material God uses to build our faith when we're working with Him.

God Builds Our Faith on Multiple Levels

Painful circumstances and situations can help build up our faith if we choose to use our faith to get through those tough times. If we don't use it, then we won't develop the strong faith God desires us to have. This whole process of exercising our faith *can* be a painful process. The saying "no pain, no gain" is appropriate as it relates to faith-building. God may not have brought you out of all your trials, but He will use them to build you up. The question is: *will you let Him?*

As we all know, challenging circumstances are inevitable; however, God wants you to use your faith to get through them. You may be thinking, "That's easy for you to say—you're not going through what I am." Well, it's not always easy for me to say either. But I believe for both of us that the greater the trials, the greater potential for using the gift of faith (and therefore, the greater the pleasure you will bring to God). Consider this verse again:

And we know that in all things [human events and circumstances] *God works for the good of those who love Him, who have been called according to His purpose* (Romans 8:28).

This is an important truth—a promise. No matter how painful, tragic, heartbreaking, or challenging a situation is, God can redeem it into something good for you. Note that this verse doesn't say, "God makes all things happen to you." It says, in spite of the circumstances, whether the result of a fallen world, someone else's actions, or even your own, God uses them to benefit those "who love Him and have been called according to His purpose."

Allow me to share a personal example of a bad situation God ultimately used for good. The first job I had after high school graduation was developing apartments with my brother in San Antonio. In 1974 and 1975 an overabundance of apartment units suddenly and dramatically drove rents down. This downturn in revenues, combined with skyrocketing utility rates, sent a large number of apartment complexes into foreclosure. It wasn't a pleasant experience for those of us who chose to build apartments during that time. This was obviously a very challenging time for me. I felt alone and vulnerable.

But as a result of that experience I learned some important lessons about real estate—especially how easy it was to inadvertently box myself into a bad situation. This was my "baptism" into real estate. Since that time I've watched other developers (who didn't have the benefit of a painful learning experience like mine) lose large sums of their own money and that of others' who trusted them. God can use our difficult experiences to teach and grow us in many ways—not only relating to our physical situation (as in this example), but in a spiritual sense as well. These challenges in life will give you needed experience and knowledge to help you in business, personal relationships and ministry as well as allowing you to relate and empathize with others experiencing similar circumstances.

ACTION & VISUALIZATION

When you encounter difficult circumstances, act in faith, hope, and trust that God has a plan for your good. This will foster a closer relationship with Him.

ACTING ON FAITH

Let's dig a little deeper by looking at the New King James translation of Hebrews 11:1:

☩ *Now **faith** is the substance of things hoped for, the evidence of things not seen* (Hebrews 11:1 NKJV).

The "things we hope for" are things that have not manifested themselves in this world. However, if you could peek into the Kingdom of God, you would find that faith is a "substance" used to make the things you hope for in this world. Therefore, this substance is evidence that the things you hope for do exist somewhere. But how do they come into existence in our world?

☩ [Jesus said] *"I will give you the keys of the Kingdom of Heaven; whatever you bind on earth will be bound in Heaven, and whatever you loose on earth will be loosed in Heaven"* (Matthew 16:19).

The things we do here on earth (good or bad) can have an affect in the Kingdom of God (Heaven) and vice versa. Do you remember reading that faith has to be combined with our actions to actually work?

☩ *...faith by itself, if it is not accompanied by **action**, is **dead*** (James 2:17).

We must *act* on faith as if what we hope for is going to manifest, otherwise our faith is dead and what we hoped for will not happen (unless it is in God's predetermined will). For faith to be alive, you must accompany it with actions that are congruent with what you are having faith for. *Faith is an action!* Your action should be lined up with what you believe because your actions have an effect on what's being "bound and loosed" in the spiritual realm, in the Kingdom of God where things we encounter in this life are being "manufactured." God sees your actions, and your actions speak louder than your words. Acting in faith on God's promises is the relationship God desires with you—and therefore doing this *pleases God!*

So how can you please God in your daily life? By walking in faith and trusting God's Word, principles, promises, and nature. This also places us on solid ground so we're able to withstand the inevitable storms that come our way.

✠ [Jesus said] *"Therefore **everyone who hears these words of Mine and puts them into practice** is like a wise man who built his house on the **rock**. The rain came down, the streams rose, and the winds blew and beat against that house; yet it did not fall, because it had its foundation on the rock"* (Matthew 7:24-25).

The faith you show in God by doing what He says gives you the ability to withstand the inevitable storms, even helps you discover *joy* in the midst of those storms.

Jesus goes on to explain what happens to someone who does not act in faith basing their life on His promises:

✠ [Jesus said] *"But **everyone who hears these words of Mine and does not put them into practice** is like a foolish man who built his house on the sand. The rain came down, the streams rose, and the winds blew and beat against that house, and it fell with a great crash"* (Matthew 7:26-27).

Jesus is saying that it is up to *us* to prepare for the storm by *acting* on His word. Moreover, when we *do* act in faith on what we know from God, we'll receive a blessing:

✝ [Jesus said] *"Now that you know these things, you will be **blessed if you do them**"* (John 13:17).

Just a reminder: when you act on God's word, that doesn't mean He'll eliminate the storms in life. Jesus says you will still have storms, but He also says that if you are obedient to His word—if you *act* in faith—the storms won't blow away your house, or say any part of your life. Hearing and acting on God's word will also bring you closer to God and allow Jesus to better *manifest* Himself in your life circumstances.

✝ [Jesus said] *"He who has My commandments and **keeps** them, it is he who loves Me. And he who loves Me will be loved by My Father, and I will love him and **manifest** Myself to him"* (John 14:21 NKJV).

ACTION & VISUALIZATION
Act in faith on God's Word.

UNSEEN THINGS

There is a concept woven throughout the Bible that states we will be blessed by God when our belief is *not* dependent on what we see.

...blessed are those who have not seen and yet have believed (John 20:29).

This is why I will remind you again of this important verse:

*We live by **faith**, not by sight* (2 Corinthians 5:7).

Living by faith means we shouldn't be overly influenced by what we see because, among other things, what we see or experience is only *temporal*. God wants you to re-establish your spiritual insight and strengthen it so you can see Him. The Bible says Adam's physical eyes were opened at the fall when his spiritual eyes become dead. God wants to build our spiritual eyes back up because as this is done we can walk more effectively by faith.

Physical things in this world come and go, but God and His spiritual truths are eternal. It may be that time now when you are experiencing a difficult circumstance, but God's truth will eventually trump it. You and God are in this together for the long haul, so that's where your vision should be focused—the *future*. The present is only a moment, but your future is an eternity.

✠ *So we fix our eyes not on what is seen, but on what is unseen. For what is seen is temporary, but what is unseen is eternal* (2 Corinthians 4:18).

You must *not* let the facts you see today overly influence you, confuse you, or rule you. Facts are real in the physical, temporal realm. God's truths are spiritual and eternal. If we believe only in facts as if they are permanent, then they likely will be; however, if we believe God's truths and walk in *faith* based on His truth, then truth *trumps* facts every time.

Living by faith will keep you on God's path, which will please Him and bring you a reward at the same time. Again an important verse you will want to hang on tight to in your spirit as you go through life:

✠ *But without faith it is impossible to please Him, for he who comes to God must believe that He is, and that He is a **rewarder** of those who **diligently** seek Him* (Hebrews 11:6 NKJV).

Every Easter, I hid eggs for our children all over *our* yard, not our neighbor's yard and not in the street where I had told our children never to go. The eggs were only where they were *supposed* to look. Sure enough when Easter morning came, my kids would enthusiastically dash out into our yard in search of the eggs. They didn't go looking in the neighbor's yard or in the street.

When they first ran into the yard they didn't see any eggs; however, even though they did not *see* the eggs my kids were excited because they had *faith* and *confidence* in their earthly father. They knew that at Easter time I was a *rewarder*. My kids knew they just had to keep looking in the area they were supposed to, and despite what they *initially* didn't see, they would *eventually* be rewarded. Eventually, they would find the eggs I had hidden.

Shouldn't we have this same *faith* and *confidence* in God our Father? The lesson is simple: if we stay on the path our heavenly Father planned for us, we can have confidence that He has left our rewards along *that* path for us to find—if not today, then tomorrow or the next day. Certainly there will be days when we come up empty; however, we should continue to search *His path* enthusiastically, knowing that God is a *rewarder* when we are on the path we are *supposed to be on*. All other paths lead to wandering and frustration.

Let me remind you again that developing your relationship with God is a *process*. Diligently seeking Him means seeking His will and intentions daily. When we know His will and intention and act on them, we receive great rewards, even though the rewards may not always be what we expect. His will and intentions are *always* good for us.

✠ *For I know the thought that I think towards you, says the Lord, thoughts of peace and not of evil, to give you a future and a hope* (Jeremiah 29:11 NKJV).

✠ [Jesus said] *"The thief does not come except to steal, to kill and to destroy. I have come that they may have life, and that they may have it more **abundantly**"* (John 10:10 NKJV).

As long as we are seeking Him and staying on His path, we can expect that God will use our experiences to perfect us in the way He desires—helping us fulfill our destiny and living that abundant life He desires for us.

ACTION & VISUALIZATION

Seek to stay on God's path at all times, and expect God to reward you along the way according to His will.

TRIALS AND TESTING OF FAITH

Not only are we called to walk in faith when faced with challenging circumstances, we're called to something else that may seem impossible at first.

✠ *Consider it pure **joy**, my brothers, whenever you face trials of many kinds, because you know that the testing of your faith develops perseverance. Perseverance must finish its work so that you may be **mature** and **complete, not lacking anything*** (James 1:2-4).

✠ *...we also **rejoice** in our **sufferings**, because we know that suffering produces perseverance; perseverance, character; and character, **hope*** (Romans 5:3-4).

Yes, you read that right. God desires that we rejoice *in* our sufferings because, among other things, they provide us with spiritual and physical development. Before going any further, please realize that we are *not* being instructed to rejoice *about* our troubles:

✠ [There is] *a time to weep and a time to laugh, a time to mourn and a time to dance...* (Ecclesiastes 3:4).

Suffering is painful; however, God has put *gifts* within our troubles that *those living in faith* can unwrap and use to *grow* their *faith, character, experiences,* and *knowledge*—but most of all grow *closer to Him.* Our joy, peace, and trust in Him helps us build up our hope to greater levels.

✠ *May the God of hope fill you with all joy and peace as you trust in Him, so that you may overflow with hope by the power of the Holy Spirit* (Romans 15:13).

You can probably imagine difficult circumstances where it might seem impossible to experience joy. That's OK to think at this point. However, you can begin to discover joy in challenging circumstances by starting small. For example, at the airline ticket counter when the attendant says, "I'm sorry, we've lost your reservation and the flight is full." Can you imagine what it would be like to maintain joy in that circumstance? You'll be surprised what happens when you do.

If you are relaxed, joyful, and going with the flow you will often discover that God has a *better* plan for your day. Sometimes you will flat out experience a miracle. And if nothing else you will definitely grow closer to God because you acted in faith and trusted God to work everything out for your good, even though you may not be fully aware of why or how He did it. As we continue to explore what it means to stay joyful, remember that it's OK to start with small circumstances and work up from there. You've probably heard that the best way to eat an elephant is one bite at a time.

People have a tendency to let their challenging circumstances get them down or influence their *outlook*. When I ask people who are going through tough times how they're doing, they invariably say, "Under the circumstances, I'm doing OK." I say to them, "Wouldn't you be better off to get out from under those circumstances? You may have to continue to live with them, but your view or *outlook* would be much better if you were on top of them rather than under them."

My point: don't let an adverse situation enslave your attitude. Your attitude and thought-life will affect your hope and your hope is essential for your faith. In turn your faith will be important in shaping the things that you will eventually run into in life which are being created in that other realm. Most importantly remember that you serve a God of redemption who has a history of restoring, healing, and promoting people in lowly places, in peril or in distress.

The Bible is overflowing with this message to you. If He has overcome the world, why should we live subject to temporal circumstances? Circumstances come and go. As believers we are eternal, we have Him in us growing as an incorruptible seed:

Who is it that overcomes the world? **Only** *he who believes that Jesus is the Son of God* (1 John 5:5).

I have told you these things, so that in Me you may have peace. In this world you will have trouble. But take heart! I have overcome the world (John 16:33).

Regardless of the reason something bad happens, God embeds in it an opportunity for you to get back to your Promised Land (redemption), both physically and spiritually. We may need some preparation before we enter it or we may need to do something before entering it. Remember, you have a promise from a loving God "that all things are working together for your good."

In the Chinese language, the word *disaster* is made up of two symbols. One conveys danger and the other is the symbol for *opportunity*. This is a good way to view our challenging circumstances—there is always a gift, an opportunity you can unwrap. When you find your barn full of horse crap, you can view it as a problem or you can see it as fertilizer for your garden.

I'm not suggesting this is easy, or even possible sometimes until after the challenging circumstance is over. In some cases it may take years to see restoration and the gift God has designed from it. However, trust God's perfect timing today and diligently choose to unwrap the opportunity in disaster. Admittedly, this is a difficult subject for our earthly minds to understand, but we'll benefit more from the gifts He offers *when* we do, and in the meantime have a better attitude while waiting in expectation of it. To help you better grasp this concept, we'll go deeper into this subject and explore many examples of this as we go through this series of books. Have faith for now!

ACTION & VISUALIZATION

Practice maintaining joy when experiencing small troubles,
so when facing bigger challenges you will be prepared.

TRUSTING GOD WITH THINGS YOU DON'T UNDERSTAND

How do we develop the ability to have joy in challenging circumstances, which we would otherwise see as major setbacks or even devastating situations? Answering this question will take time and trust as you grow in your relationship with God. There are many things that cannot be described in this book. But that's part of God's plan—you'll understand and accept these truths better when God is the teacher, *not me.*

Remember that the core truth of this life of faith is your relationship with *God.* Though pastors and books and other sources can help you discover new truths, it's ultimately *your direct relationship with God* that allows you to grow into the person God wants you to be. Talk to God when things happen you don't understand. Then *listen.* Be open for God's answer and know that it will come in His time and according to His plan. Be open and prepared—the answer could surprise you and cause you to miss it!

Remember, from your vantage point, you only see a small part of God's overall grand plan, which is too complex for our human minds to comprehend.

✠ *"For My thoughts are not your thoughts, neither are your ways My ways," declares the Lord. "As the heavens are higher than the earth, so are My ways higher than your ways and My thoughts than your thoughts"* (Isaiah 55:8-9).

All of science and man's knowledge accumulated over thousands of years by billions of people still have not given us a full understanding of how God created our complex physical bodies to function. So it's not likely we, apart from Him, are going to know how He has our life planned out.

To help you through your lack of understanding, God will sometimes give you glimpses of the future *beyond* your current trial and tribulation. Having faith in these previews can make it much easier to know joy while you're still in the midst of your challenging circumstances. Also, you already know your ultimate destiny—Heaven, where you will become the image and likeness of God, spending an *eternity with Him.*

✦ *...we are looking forward to a new Heaven and a new earth, the home of righteousness* (2 Peter 3:13).

This thought in Second Peter alone can help you keep the temporal challenges in proper perspective. I believe if you really knew and fully understood your future, you'd be smiling right now. I believe we have a hard time hanging onto joy and a victor's mentality in difficult times *not* because of the things that are happening, but because we don't fully understand *why* these things are happening. If we understood why, then we might better exhibit an unusual faith to *lift* us above our circumstances. Look at what the apostle Paul wrote to the Colossian church:

✦ *...we have not stopped praying for you and asking God to **fill you with knowledge of His will through all spiritual wisdom and understanding.** And we pray this in order that you may live a life worthy of the Lord and may please Him in every way: bearing fruit in every good work, growing in the knowledge of God, being strengthened with all power according to His glorious might so that you may have great endurance and patience, and joyfully giving thanks to the Father, who has qualified you to share in the inheritance of the saints in the kingdom of light* (Colossians 1:9-12).

When we don't understand—when faith is difficult—this is part of God's refining fire. It shows our humanity and our need for a Savior. Peter, who followed and lived with Christ, mistakenly believed he could better survive some particularly difficult circumstances on his own. Though at the time circumstances seemed like they were going out of control with Jesus' arrest and impending crucifixion, God had the situation *perfectly* under control. Through the trials he experienced, Peter's faith grew and his more-developed faith eventually allowed him to do some unusual and dramatic things for God.

There will be times you don't fully understand what is happening and in those scariest and most confusing moments, your only *comfort* may be the knowledge of your eternal life which God has placed in you. Have faith in His love for you.

✢ *He has made everything beautiful in its time. He has also set eternity in the hearts of men; yet they cannot fathom what God has done from the beginning to end* (Ecclesiastes 3:11).

Pray often that you might grow in the knowledge and understanding of God's will especially as it relates to dealing with challenging circumstances that enter your life. This is also a good thing to pray for your loved ones.

ACTION & VISUALIZATION
Even when you don't fully understand the reason,
act in faith when facing challenging circumstances.

GOD LAYS A FOUNDATION FOR YOUR FAITH

Our faith can also be built up by studying God's omnipotence and omniscience. Let's start at the beginning:

✢ *...And there was evening, and there was morning—the first day* (Genesis 1:5).

✢ *...And there was evening, and there was morning—the second day* (Genesis 1:8).

✝ *...And there was evening, and there was morning—the third day* (Genesis 1:13).

✝ *...And there was evening, and there was morning—the fourth day* (Genesis 1:19).

✝ *...And there was evening, and there was morning—the fifth day* (Genesis 1:23).

✝ *God saw all that **he had made**, and it was very good. And there was evening, and there was morning—the sixth day. Thus the heavens and earth were **completed** in their vast array* (Genesis 1:31-2:1).

The very first chapter of the first book of the Bible demonstrates quite clearly that God created *everything* within the heavens and earth. This foundational chapter can act as a strong foundation for your daily living faith if you truly believe in it. Though there are many theories about the actual timeframe, Genesis' account is six days—I don't see how God could have made it clearer that it was six *literal* 24-hour days. To leave no doubt, God separated each day in the Bible with an evening and a morning. Indeed *every* time in the Bible the word *day* (Yom) follows a numerical number it means a 24-hour period.

Imagine if you had complete *confidence* in this account of the creation of the whole universe as we know it. How would that change everyday trials for you? Those seemingly insurmountable troubles? Wouldn't you have to say, *"Certainly, a God who can create the world and everything in it in six days can handle any problem I might face!"* By remembering the power God had to create *all* things in *just* six days, you can be confident that God can and will deliver on His promises to you.

Some Christians believe that the Creation story should not be taken literally or that you can believe that God somehow used evolution to make His creation within the context of what the Bible says. However, the Bible in both the Old and New Testament says God spoke the world into existence.

⊕ *By the word of the Lord were the heavens made, their starry host by the breath of His mouth...For He **spoke and it came to be**;* (Psalm 33:6-9).

⊕ *By faith we understand that the universe was formed at God's **command**, so that what is seen was **not** made out of what **was visible*** (Hebrews 11:3).

On the other hand, the evolution theory purports that all was made over long periods of time, random chance, and natural processes. Does this sound like a description of the same thing? Let's look deeper. God says He began earth's creation with water, while evolution says a fiery ball from an explosion came first. How about the order of creation? God says He created the earth first and then the stars on the 4th day, while evolution says the order was reverse. God says He created the birds first then the reptiles on the sixth day, while evolution says the order was reverse.

There is no way the evolution theory will fly with the Bible account. In fact, flight itself, from an evolutionary standpoint, is impossible because from a purely scientific perspective flight requires too many complex things to occur *all* at the *same time*. Among them a unique light bone structure (using honeycomb design *not* found in other animals), a unique joint structure, unique muscles, perfectly aerodynamically designed wings, an interlocking but flexible feather design and completely unique lung design allowing for maximum lung capacity to support the extra oxygen requirement to the blood for energy. All birds and only birds have a put-through system of air going continuously through the lung system instead of the in and out dead-end system found in all other animals.[1]

Again *all* these mutations would be required to happen at the same time according to the law of natural selection. If only *one* did not occur in that mutation there could be no flight and the mutations would vanish because it did not serve a useful purpose, that's the law of natural selection.[2] I believe if you took the time to study all the additional detail that would need to happen for birds to fly you would agree that the complex combination would be impossible to be achieved by random chance even *once*. Remember though, it would have had to occur three times: once for birds, once for mammals, and once for insects.

There is no way you can believe that God used evolution to create the world if you believe the Bible to be the inspired Word of God. There are only two ways the world and everything in it came about—creation by the Creator as recorded in Genesis or evolution by man's theory. One is right and one is *wrong*.

The most important question raised when trying to combine evolution with the Genesis account: what came first, sin or death? Again we see an irreconcilable difference in the two outlooks. In the evolution model death came first because you had to have billions of years of death to create man and only once created could man then sin. However, Paul in Romans says:

⊕ *Therefore, just as sin entered the world through one man, and death through sin, and in this way death came to all men, because all sinned* (Romans 5:12).

The order is clear here—first man, then sin, and then death. In the evolution model God would have had to give the creation death rather than man (who brought it about by disobeying God's will). And then how could you make sense of God's description of His new creation?

✠ *God saw all that he had made, and **it was very good**. And there was evening, and there was morning—the sixth day. Thus the heavens and earth were **completed** in their vast array* (Genesis 1:31–2:1).

If His creation was achieved through billions of years of death and decay then how could God have said it was *very good*? He couldn't—and didn't.

Though believing theories other than the literal six-day creation doesn't take away anyone's salvation, I believe it is clearly God's intent that we believe He *did* create the world in six days. In so doing our faith is strengthened, and our strong actions of faith please God.

Whether you believe God created everything in six days or in an evolutionary process lasting hundreds of billions of years, you will have to rely on faith. No human witnessed creation. However, we Christians do have a witness—God. His account is written in the Bible. When you match scientific evidence against God's account and the evolutionists' theory, there is actually a better scientific fit with the biblical account of what happened. It's vastly more logical and compatible with scientific facts.

I strongly encourage as part of your supplemental reading that you examine the *scientific case* for creation science. I believe you will see, based on the *evidence*, that the "six day creation model" is substantially *more credible* than the evolution model. Seeing this for yourself will build your confidence in the literal interpretation of creation. Taking this on just faith, however, will not build your faith as much as doing your *own study* and coming to your *own conclusions* based on science. When you see for yourself the unbelievable complexity and beauty in God's design of everything He made, it will *encourage* your faith because:

✝ *The heavens* [His creation] *declare the glory of God; the skies proclaim the work of His hands* (Psalm 19:1).

Your built-up faith will give you more freedom and power in your walk with God as well as a closer relationship. Also, it is important that we have a clear and concise answer for our faith and beliefs.

✝ *...Always be prepared to give an answer to everyone...for the hope you have* (1 Peter 3:15).

Therefore it is important you do your own study of this all-important question of how our very existence came about. Don't take someone else's word or listen to so-called experts. It is important your answer does not make God's Word a lie, for how then can the world believe God's other promises?

✝ *First of all, you must understand that in the last days sufferers will come, scoffing and following their own evil desires. They will say, "Where is this 'coming' he promised? Ever since our fathers died, everything goes on as it has since the beginning of creation." But they* **deliberately forget** *that long ago by God's* **word** *the heavens existed and the earth was formed out of* **water** *and by* **water.** *By these waters also the world of that time was deluged and destroyed* [Noah's flood]. *By the* **same word** *the present heavens and earth are reserved for fire, being kept for the day of judgment, and destruction of ungodly men* (2 Peter 3:3-7).

By now you probably see how important it is for you to spend some time studying. A great book on this subject is *The Amazing Story of Creation: From Science and the Bible* by Duane T. Gish (Master Books Publisher). Another good book is *The New Answer Book* by Ken Ham (Master Books Publisher). Other creation science material can be found at: www.icr.org and www.creationevidence.org and www.answersingenesis.com. Two of these groups operate museums where you can actually see evidence that supports the six day creation model.

It is important that you view Genesis and the other books of the Bible as accurate accounts of God's history with us. These accounts are designed to give you knowledge and encouragement—and to build your faith in God. God showed His power through regular people like you and me for edification, knowledge, and encouragement in an effort to build up our faith. Throughout the Book of Exodus, God told the Israelites to tell their children about the great and powerful things He had done. We are His children, too. Therefore we should learn from these accounts in the Bible's rich history of people who lived by faith.

If Adam and Eve's story were just a fairy tale, then who made the choice to violate God's will and bring evil into the world? The foundation for the entire Gospel message is found in the story of Adam and Eve's creation and downfall. Jesus spoke of them in Mark 10:6. Indeed, Genesis is the most quoted book in the Bible by Jesus Himself. Here is what Jesus said about Moses who was the author of Genesis:

If you believed Moses, you would believe Me, for he wrote about Me. But since you do not believe what he wrote, how are you going to believe what I say (John 5:46-47).

Out of Genesis comes the principles of marriage, sin, death, the Sabbath (day of rest), and even the reason Jesus had to die on the Cross. Satan knows that if you can undermine the foundation of a building, you can collapse the entire building. A believer's foundation is the Bible. The Bible's foundation is the Book of Genesis.

✠ *When the foundations are being destroyed, what can the righteous do?* (Psalm 11:3)

I believe it is critical to trust what God says to us in His Word, so your faith can be built on the most solid foundation.

ACTION & VISUALIZATION

Knowing and believing in God's Word
will give you power to
trust Him in every situation.

WALKING TOWARD GOD

Walking is a two-step process. First you move your right leg, then your left, as you make movement forward and so on. Walking toward God is essentially the same in that our first step is an action of faith—this allows you to begin, to enter into a relationship. The first step of faith is very important, but if you are going to achieve intimacy and closeness within the relationship, you have to go many steps further.

The next step is to start removing whatever blocks and hinders you from achieving intimacy. Then your next step again is faith—diligently putting your faith into action *every day*—to *habitually* take step after step of faith from the first step to the last:

✝ *For in the gospel a righteousness **from** God is revealed, a righteousness that is **by** faith from the first to last, just as it is written: "The righteous will live by faith"* (Romans 1:17).

Faith should always be the lead step as you journey through life. It was by Abraham's faith *not* his virtuous living that he became righteous in God's eyes. Likewise, our faith in Jesus was our first step—for this is the only avenue that brings us into right standing with God, not our good works or virtuous living. When our relationship with God is reestablished through faith alone, does God completely reshift His emphasis to grow the relationship on virtue alone? Of course not, though you will find many Christians and churches making that their primary focus—primarily focused on exhorting Christians to stop sinning. In essence their message becomes, "Stop making God mad!" But, not making Him mad isn't necessarily pleasing Him. Remember:

✝ *For we walk by faith not by sight* (2 Corinthians 5:7 NKJV).

✝ *And without faith it is impossible to please God...* (Hebrews 11:6).

✝ *Does God give you his Spirit and work miracles among you because you observe the law, or **because you believe what you heard** [God's Word]? Consider Abraham: "He believed God, and it was credited to him as righteousness." Understand, then, that those who believe are children of Abraham. The Scripture foresaw that God would justify the Gentiles by faith, and announced the gospel in advance to Abraham: "All nations will be blessed through you." So those who have faith are blessed along with Abraham, the man of faith. All who* *rely on observing the law are under a curse, for it is written: "Cursed is everyone who does not continue to do everything written in the Book of the Law." Clearly no one is justified before God by the law, because, "The righteous will **live by faith**"* (Galatians 3:5-11).

Our greatest mandate is to use faith in everything we do and continue to walk in faith diligently, going beyond our first step of faith which will sometimes lead us beyond our comfort zone. I believe God is calling us to this greater goal—to continue stepping in faith above and beyond our first step of faith, salvation.

I am not saying the effort to quit sinning is not essential in cultivating an intimate walk with God. After all, you must do this to conform yourself to the image and likeness of God. Also, sin in your life is a poison that kills many areas of your life—it counter-acts faith. Unresolved sin also limits you, keeping you imprisoned in areas which results in death, sickness, disease, depression, poverty, literal imprisonment, etc.

So here's the point, walking requires both legs. Continuously taking steps of faith toward God multiplies faith, building it even stronger, which in turn pleases God. Indeed, unless you strengthen your faith, you will crumble under the pressure of the sins—that which holds you captive.

Remember the Israelites whom God brought out of their slavery from Egypt in a marvelous way through the parting of the Red Sea? God fed them daily with manna from Heaven, provided water from rocks, and much more. Yet despite all this, they were still afraid and at times wanted to go back to Egypt—back to captivity. To them, bondage was a familiar surrounding, safer then trusting God's promises in the face of an unseen and unknown future.

This is the same with our walk. We were not freed from the Egyptians, but from sin; however, we wind up voluntarily going back into bondage. Sin is not the only thing we have a hard time letting go of. There is our general lack and loss of freedoms. While conditions in our life may be bad and we may be suffering from lack, we are used to living with it—it's *familiar*. So when God speaks to us to have faith for something great—to strike a rock for water, to blow a horn and shout to bring down walls in life, to step out of the boat and walk on the water, to love somebody unlovable, it can be hard to trust God and take steps toward a future we can't physically see. However, it is through those steps that our faith is built up, manifesting the freedoms we've been offered.

You also need a strong faith because some sin is buried *deep*; without a strong faith it can be impossible to dislodge. God's presence must become vivid in your life so you involve Him in your every move. As you strive to construct a solid foundation for your relationship with God remember:

✝ *Unless the Lord builds the house, its builders labor vain...* (Psalm 127:1).

You alone will *never* be able to get sin out of your life and conform yourself to the image and likeness of God. There are strongholds in your body and mind that are like impenetrable fortresses with high walls. The Israelites needed God's plan for victory to take possession of these areas in their Promised Land—and so do you. Just like the Israelites, it is your actions in faith that will make you victorious. As your faith grows, God becomes clearer and clearer in your everyday life. As His presence becomes more *evident* in your everyday life, the following verse will have more meaning and *impact* in your life.

✝ *Nothing in all creation is hidden from God's sight. Everything is uncovered and laid bare before the eyes of Him to whom we must give account* (Hebrews 4:13).

If His presence were more *real* to you in your everyday life when temptations came, wouldn't it be *easier* to resist them knowing confidentially He is looking over your shoulder at the time? Your built-up faith will help you remove sin from your life. Indeed, your built-up faith will help you remove many unwanted things in your life. In your walk toward an intimate relationship with God, make sure each alternating step is a step of faith. Those alternating steps in faith will keep you looking good in God's eyes until you can become who He desires you to be.

ACTION & VISUALIZATION
Lead with a step of faith each alternating step in life.

EXERCISE YOUR FAITH

God wants us to take what measure of faith He has given us and *use* it, therein growing its strength. This gift of faith is just like the talents and other abilities God gives. He desires to build and multiply them through our actions. Jesus expressed this concept in a story He told His disciples:

✠ *Again, it will be like a man going on a journey, who called his servants and entrusted his property to them. To one he gave five talents of money, to another two talents, and to another one talent, each according to his ability. Then he went on his journey. The man who had received the five talents went at once and put his money to work and gained five more. So also, the one with the two talents gained two more. But the man who had received the one talent went off, dug a hole in the ground and hid his master's money. After a long time the master of those servants returned and settled accounts with them. The man who had received the five talents brought the other five. "Master," he said, "you entrusted me with five talents. See, I have gained five more." His master replied, "Well done, good and faithful servant! You have been faithful with a few things; I will put you in charge of many things. Come and share your master's happiness!" The man with the two talents also came. "Master," he said, "you entrusted me with two talents; see, I have gained two more." His master replied, "Well done, good and faithful servant! You have been faithful with a few things; I will put you in charge of many things. Come and share your master's happiness!" Then the man who had received the one talent came. "Master," he said, "I knew that you are a hard man, harvesting where you have not sown and gathering where you have not scattered seed. So I was afraid and went out and hid your talent in the ground. See, here is what belongs to you." His master replied, "You wicked, lazy servant! So you knew that I harvest where I have not sown and gather where I have not scattered seed? Well then, you should have put my money on deposit with the bankers, so that when I returned I would have received it back with interest." "Take the talent from him and give it to the one who has the ten talents. For everyone who has will be given more and he will have an abundance. Whoever does not have, even what he has will be taken from him. And throw that worthless servant outside, into the darkness, where there will be weeping and gnashing of teeth"* (Matthew 25:14-30).

This is sort of like the "use it or lose it" concept regarding exercise. When you stop using muscles they will grow smaller. Think about how this applies to your faith. Wouldn't you rather hear God tell you, "Well done good and faithful servant; you have used your faith so I will give you more" rather than, "Take from him what he has and cast him into the darkness." It was *fear* that caused the unprofitable servant to bury his talent and choose not to make an investment. Fear is also what keeps us from exercising our faith. The good news is that faith, like muscles, can start being built up at any time by your *actions*. How are you investing or exercising your specific God-given faith and talents?

ACTION & VISUALIZATION

Look for opportunities to use and exercise your faith.

HAVE FAITH IN WHO GOD IS

When, despite our circumstances, we come to God in faith, our faith pleases God—giving us the opportunity to fully experience Him and His power. We see this in many instances in the Bible. Here are just a few. Note the role that faith plays in each.

☦ *Some men brought to Him a paralytic, lying on a mat. When Jesus saw their **faith**, He said to the paralytic, "Take heart, son; your sins are forgiven." But so that you may know that the Son of Man has authority on earth to forgive sins..." Then He said to the paralytic, "Get up, take your mat and go home." And the man got up and went home* (Matthew 9:2,6-7).

☦ *A Canaanite woman from that vicinity came to Him* [Jesus], *crying out, "Lord, Son of David, have mercy on me! My daughter is suffering terribly from demon-possession." Then Jesus answered, "Woman, you have great **faith**! Your request is granted." And her daughter was healed from that very hour* (Matthew 15:22,28).

✟ *Jesus said to the woman, "Your **faith** has saved you; go in peace"* (Luke 7:50).

✟ *Then He [Jesus] said to him, "Rise and go; your **faith** has made you well"* (Luke 17:19).

✟ *Jesus said to him [blind man], "Receive your sight; your **faith** has healed you"* (Luke 18:42).

✟ *There a centurion's servant, whom his master valued highly, was sick and about to die. The centurion heard of Jesus and sent some elders of the Jews to Him, asking Him to come and heal his servant. When they came to Jesus, they pleaded earnestly with Him, "This man deserves to have you do this, because he loves our nation and has built our synagogue." So Jesus went with them. He was not far from the house when the centurion sent friends to say to Him: "Lord, don't trouble Yourself, for I do not deserve to have You come under my roof. That is why I did not even consider myself worthy to come to You. But say the word, and my servant will be healed. For I myself am a man under authority, with soldiers under me. I tell this one, 'Go,' and he goes; and that one, 'Come,' and he comes. I say to my servant, 'Do this,' and he does it." When Jesus heard this, He was amazed at him, and turning to the crowd following Him, He said, "I tell you, I have not found such great **faith** even in Israel." Then the men who had been sent returned to the house and found the servant well* (Luke 7:2-10).

Imagine what it would be like to have Jesus marvel at how you have built up your *faith*! As you can tell, there are many examples in the Bible when someone's faith *moves* God to act. There are also many examples in the Bible when a *lack* of faith discourages God. In the beginning of Mark chapter 6, Jesus is in Nazareth where He grew up as a young boy. They knew Jesus as the carpenter's son, and did not know Jesus for who He was—the Savior and Son of God. Read what happens:

Jesus left there and went to his hometown, accompanied by His disciples. When the Sabbath came, He began to teach in the synagogue, and many who heard Him were amazed. "Where did this man get these things?" they asked. "What's this wisdom that has been given Him, that He even does miracles! Isn't this the carpenter? Isn't this Mary's son and the brother of James, Joseph, Judas and Simon? Aren't His sisters here with us?" And they took offense at Him. Jesus said to them, "Only in his hometown, among his relatives and in his own house is a prophet without honor." **He could not do any miracles there, except lay His hands on a few sick people and heal them.** *And He was amazed at their* **lack of faith** (Mark 6:1-6).*

Later in the same chapter of Mark, Jesus crosses the Sea of Galilee to Gennesaret where it says the people recognized Him for who He was—the Messiah:

When they had crossed over, they landed at Gennesaret and anchored there. As soon as they got out of the boat, people **recognized Jesus.** *[Acting in faith] They ran throughout that whole region, and carried the sick on mats to wherever they heard He was. And wherever He went—into villages, towns or countryside—they placed the sick in the marketplaces.* **They begged Him to let them touch even the edge of His cloak, and all who touched Him were healed** (Mark 6:53-56).

Because they had faith in who Jesus was, many were healed. They exhibited this by wanting to touch the edge of his cloak or "tallit." To fully understand this verse it's important to know the context or customs of the day. A tallit was a rectangle scarf-like garment that hung down from around the neck; however, it was wider so that when praying they could put it over there heads to create a tent-like effect, a holy place to meet God. At the hem of the cloak or tallit on the four corners there is a tassel (tzitzit) made of eight strands with five knots which represented all of God's commandments and the names of God. In addition, one thread in the tassel was blue which represented the Messiah. So the full manifestation and embodiment of God was represented by these tassels. When praying they were to hold onto these tassels as a reminder of God and His word to them.

 The Lord said to Moses, "Speak to the Israelites and say to them: 'Throughout the generations to come you are to make tassels on the corners of your garments, with a blue cord on each tassel. You will have these tassels to look at and so you will remember all the commands of the Lord, that you may obey them and not prostitute yourselves by going after the lusts of your own hearts and eyes'" (Numbers 15:37-39).

When one held the corners of their tallit, it created wings and they knew from prophecy that in the wings of the Messiah there was healing.

 But for you who revere my name, the sun of righteousness will rise with healing in its wings...(Malachi 4:2).

Their faith in Jesus for who He is produced the result of many being healed when He crossed over to Gennesaret. You see this same faith again in the story of the woman with an issue of blood.

⊕ *A large crowd followed and pressed around Him. And a woman was there who had been subject to bleeding for twelve years. She had suffered a great deal under the care of many doctors and had spent all she had, yet instead of getting better she grew worse. When she heard about Jesus, she came up behind Him in the crowd and touched His cloak [tallit], because she thought, "**If I just touch His clothes [tallit], I will be healed.**" Immediately her bleeding stopped and she felt in her body that she was **freed** from her suffering. At once Jesus realized that power had gone out from Him. He turned around in the crowd and asked, "Who touched my clothes?" "You see the people crowding **against You**," His disciples answered, "and yet You can ask, 'Who touched me?'"* (Mark 5:24-31)

Having an issue with blood for *12 years* would have made her an outcast. The most important thing to note is that although there were many people touching and crowding around Jesus, only one received healing power from Him. She was not one whom Jesus had a predetermination to heal, but because of her faith, and taking action to reach out to Him, her faith drew healing power from Him. In the world and even churches today, many people are crowded around Jesus touching Him; however, they are not receiving His full power because they are not reaching out in persistent faith to Him as their healer, provider, comforter, strengthener, etc.

Many people perceive God incorrectly so they don't experience all that He has to offer. It is important to have faith in His attributes for that is how you unwrap them. The parable of the talents illustrates how the servants' perceptions of God caused them to act in a way that blesses two of them with the fullness of God, while the one with the wrong perception of God gets nothing but trouble. What was this servant's perception of God that caused him to come up empty handed?

✝ *Then the man who had received the one talent came. "Master," he said, "I knew that you are a **hard** man, harvesting where you have not sown and gathering where you have not scattered seed. So I was **afraid** and went out and hid your talent in the ground..."* (Matthew 25:24-25).

It's important for you to have faith in God's character and attributes. Our faith in God begins with the belief that God *is* love and therefore can only exude *love*. Our faith in His unfailing love pleases God:

✝ *His [God's] pleasure is not in the strength of the horse, nor His delight in the legs of man; the Lord delights in those who fear Him, who put their hope in His **unfailing love*** (Psalm 147:10-11).

Although God is a just God, He is not a *hard* God—we should not be *afraid* of Him. He is a God of love and mercy, and we are to trust in His unfailing love and *power*.

✝ *Wealth and honor come from You; You are the ruler of all things. In Your hands are strength and power to exalt and give strength to all* (1 Chronicles 29:12).

✝ [A prophet warning King Amaziah that God would not be with him if he went into a particular battle said] *"Even if you go and fight courageously in battle, God will overthrow you before the enemy, for God has the power to help or to overthrow"* (2 Chronicles 25:8).

You also can trust that God is *everywhere* and *knows everything*.

✟ *Acknowledge and take to heart this day that the Lord is God in Heaven above and on earth below...*(Deuteronomy 4:39).

✟ *Nothing in all creation is hidden from God's sight...* (Hebrews 4:13).

✟ *Does He* [God] *not see my ways and count my **every** step?* (Job 31:4)

✟ *His* [God's] *eyes are on the ways of men; He sees their **every** step* (Job 34:21).

✟ *Great is our Lord and mighty in power; His understanding has **no** limit* (Psalm 147:5).

And you can have faith in the truth that there are *no limits to what God can do.*

✟ *I know that You can do **all things**; no plan of Yours can be thwarted* (Job 42:2).

✟ *Our God is in Heaven; He does **whatever** pleases Him* (Psalms 115:3).

✠ *The Lord does* **whatever** *pleases Him, in the heavens and on the earth...* (Psalms 135:6).

✠ *For* **nothing** *is impossible with God* (Luke 1:37).

Having faith in each of these attributes of God will help *manifest* that attribute into your own life. Of course the opposite is also true, acting in a lack of faith in these attributes will cause you to miss out on the full benefits they can bring you. Finally, the more you know and trust in Jesus, the more He will bring His supernatural power into your life. Just like all the other gifts, you must unwrap faith and use it to ignite and dramatically affect your life. Most of all, as you grow in faith, God will be pleased.

✠ *"If you can?" said Jesus. "Everything is possible for him who believes"* (Mark 9:23).

✠ *...My righteous one will live by faith. And if he shrinks back, I will not be pleased with him* (Hebrews 10:38).

MEDITATION POINT

Walk through life in faith trusting your heavenly Father's loving intentions for you.

Go to Chapter 6 in the Study Guide section on page 299.

ENDNOTES

1. Michael Denton, *Evolution: A Theory in Crisis.* (Chevy Chase, MD: Adler & Adler, Publishers Inc., 1985), 210-212.

2. Ibid.

Chapter 7

GIFT #3—FAITH (PART 2)

HOW CAN YOU STRENGTHEN YOUR FAITH?

Before you begin to read, pray that the Holy Spirit
will give you understanding and application.

✠ [Jesus said] *"I tell you the truth, if you have **faith** as small as a mustard seed, you can say to this mountain, 'Move from here to there' and it will move. Nothing will be impossible for you"* (Matthew 17:20).

Do you believe Jesus' words in Matthew 17:20? Can our faith truly be limitless? If so, how does that change your life? If you have ever watched a spider crawling, perhaps you've noticed that some spiders can move surprisingly fast, their swift legs coordinated in a sweeping motion, moving gracefully along the ground. What if the spider's eight legs moved in different directions, some forward, some backward, and others sideways? The spider would go nowhere.

✠ *Faith by itself, if it is not accompanied by **action**, is dead* (James 2:17).

Just as the spider must coordinate all eight legs to move toward a goal, we must line up *all* our actions to have a *functioning* faith—a unified faith in forward motion. Remember that you are made up of spirit, mind, and body. These three aspects of our make up need to move in harmony, in one cohesive direction toward what Jesus calls "mountain moving" (limitless) faith. The necessary direction is, of course, to move in sync with the will of God. Let's take a closer look at what the apostle Paul wrote to the Roman church about the acceptance of that initial gift of life:

That if you confess with your mouth, "Jesus is Lord," and believe in your heart that God raised Him from the dead, you will be saved. For it is with your heart that you believe and are justified, and it is with your mouth that you confess and are saved (Romans 10:9-10).

Paul says that to have "saving faith" we must align our *verbal* confession to what we believe in our *heart* to receive eternal life. *Living faith* works the same way. To move mountains we must unify faith and action, our *words* and our *heart*. We might be able to confess anything, but we can't hide our heart's true feelings from God.

✝ *...but God knows your hearts* (Luke 16:15).

✝ *...but the Lord looks at the heart* (1 Samuel 16:7).

✝ *...for the Lord searches every heart...*(1 Chronicles 28:9).

✝ *The crucible for silver and the furnace for gold, but the Lord tests the heart* (Proverbs 17:3).

What's in your heart? Is it in alignment with what you're saying? Is it aligned with your desires? Your actions? God's will? What needs to change—your heart, your words, your actions? All three?

To get mountain-moving faith we need to learn to trust God completely, taking hold of hope over doubt.

✠ *But when he [you] asks, he must **believe** and **not doubt**, because he who doubts is like a wave of the sea, blown and tossed by the wind* (James 1:6).

✠ *Let us hold unswervingly to the hope we **profess,** for He who promised is faithful* (Hebrews 10:23).

✠ *Trust in the Lord with all your heart...*(Proverbs 3:5).

Pockets of *doubt* will leave you directionless, and open to paths that are *not* aligned with God's will. To shed doubts, repeatedly confess your hope as if you believe it will happen. Your thought life is powerful; it can connect you to fear or build within you a fearless faith. You must align your mind, desires, heart, words, and actions with your hope in God. This is why the Bible says:

✠ *For as he thinks in his heart, so is he...* (Proverbs 23:7 NKJV).

✠ *...the Lord searches every **heart** and understands every motive behind the thoughts...* (1 Chronicles 28:9).

Our words are *powerful* and have a *big* impact on our lives. Consider this:

✟ *If anyone considers himself religious and yet does not keep a tight rein on his tongue, he deceives himself and his religion is worthless* (James 1:26).

✟ *Reckless words pierce like a sword, but the tongue of the wise brings healing* (Proverbs 92:18).

✟ *He who guards his mouth and his tongue keeps himself from calamity* (Proverbs 21:23).

✟ *The mouth of the righteous man utters wisdom, and his tongue speaks what is just* (Psalm 37:30).

✟ *Or take ships as an example. Although they are so large and are driven by strong winds, they are steered by a very small rudder wherever the pilot wants to go. Likewise the tongue is a small part of the body, but it makes great boasts. Consider what a great forest is set on fire by a small spark* (James 3:4-5).

The words you say to others as well as to yourself have great power over your physical *and* spiritual life. Words can change the direction of your life—for the better or for the worse. Consider how God used words to create all things in this world including us.

✠ *And God **said,** "Let there be light;" and there was light...* (Genesis 1:3).

God went on to *speak* each thing He created into existence. There is creative power in the spoken word. This is also confirmed in the New Testament:

✠ *By faith we understand that the universe was formed at God's **command**, so that what is seen was **not** made out of what was visible* (Hebrews 11:3).

Just as God spoke light into existence and all other things into existence from things not seen, we, on a smaller scale, are "creating things" in our own life daily. Despite what you believed up until now, the circumstances you encounter in your earthly life are *not* made from things that are visible in this world. Remember, they begin in the unseen world where faith is a substance.

Outside of God's specific will, the things that are going to happen to us are the things we *believe* and *say* are going to happen or the result of things set in motion by the invisible laws of our universe. Words spoken in *faith*, and therein believed by the heart, can influence the spirit realm. Faith is a substance in the spiritual realm that affects the physical. Indeed, I like to say that godly desires mixed with faith are memories of the future.

How could living out this idea truly affect your prayer life? Do you pray, then believe, then live out your life with faith in what you are praying for? Do you speak words of faith over your children? Your marriage? Your finances? Your next meeting?

Just saying positive affirmations from God's Word can build on your overall faith.

✠ *I can do everything through Him* [God] *who gives me strength* (Philippians 4:13).

✠ *...Do not grieve, for the joy of the Lord is your strength* (Nehemiah 8:10).

✠ *...If God is for us who can be against us?* (Romans 8:31)

There is real power you can lay hold of with this sort of faith. Don't get me wrong. I am not saying you can just say to the rain "stop" and it will stop. Your words must not be contradictory to God's will. However, Jesus made it clear that our faith can accomplish limitless things. Believe in your heart and speak it forth with your mouth—you are equipped with life-changing, supernatural power.

Are you conscious of the words that you are speaking over your life? Indeed, carelessness can lead to unintentionally speaking negative things into your life, and into the life of others. As much as possible, speak positive words and positive affirmations into your life and those around you.

✠ *Do not let any unwholesome talk come out of your mouths, but only what is helpful for building others up according to their needs, that it may benefit those who listen* (Ephesians 4:29).

ACTION & VISUALIZATION

Align your words and your heart, and speak positive things into your life and the lives of others.

THE POWER OF THE WORD

You will remember from Chapter 2 that Jesus Christ came as the Word:

✟ *In the beginning was the Word, and the Word was with God, and the Word was God. ...The Word became flesh and made His dwelling among us. We have seen His glory, the glory of the One and Only, Who came from the Father, full of grace and truth* (John 1:1,14).

This power of the spoken word is how Jesus Christ sustains all things, including our spirit and our life:

✟ *The Son is the radiance of God's glory and the exact representation of His being, sustaining all things by His powerful word...* (Hebrews 1:3).

✟ *...man does not live on bread alone but on every word that comes from the mouth of the Lord* (Deuteronomy 8:3).

In the previous chapter you learned that the catalyst to get the most benefit from the Word is to combine it with your faith.

✟ *...the message they heard was of no value to them, because those who heard did not combine it with faith* (Hebrews 4:2).

✟ [God said] *so is My word that goes out from My mouth: It will not return to Me empty, but will accomplish what I desire and achieve the purpose for which I sent it* (Isaiah 55:11).

As God's creation, made in His image and likeness, we have access to our Creator's power and authority. Though our words spoken in faith can never trump God's word, the Bible suggests ways in which that power can be enacted. Let's look back at God's original plan:

✠ *God blessed them and said to them, "Be fruitful and increase in number; fill the earth and subdue it. Rule over the fish of the sea and the birds of the air and over every living creature that moves on the ground" (Genesis 1:28).*

We temporarily lost this authority to satan when man sinned. Jesus came on our behalf and took back that authority, then passed along this authority to us.

✠ *Then Jesus came to them and said, "All authority in Heaven and on earth has been given to Me" (Matthew 28:18).*

✠ *[Jesus said] "I will give you the keys to the Kingdom of Heaven; whatever you bind on earth will be bound in Heaven, and whatever you loose on earth will be loosed in Heaven" (Matthew 16:19).*

Jesus gave a special authority to His disciples.

✠ *Jesus said, "Peace be with you! As the Father has sent me, I am sending you," And with that He breathed on them and said, "Receive the Holy Spirit. If you forgive anyone his sins, they are forgiven; if you do not forgive them, they are not forgiven" (John 20:21-23).*

You have already learned that we regained authority over our lives and our world when we were broken free of sin. Therefore our tongue can have a life and death effect on us and others both physically and spiritually.

✙ *The tongue has the power of life and death...* (Proverbs 18:21).

✙ *The tongue that brings healing is a tree of life, but a deceitful tongue crushes the spirit* (Proverbs 15:4).

✙ *He who guards his lips guards his life, but he who speaks rashly will come to ruin* (Proverbs 13:3).

✙ *Whoever would love life and see good days must keep his tongue from evil and his lips from deceitful speech* (1 Peter 3:10).

✙ *Avoid godless chatter, because those who indulge in it will become more and more ungodly* (2 Timothy 2:16).

Look at some of the faithless statements we make: "Nothing good ever happens to me," or "I can't get a break," or "I can't get anywhere because of my lack of education," or even "My childhood experiences create too many problems for me." Does this sound like someone who has been given power and authority by God the Creator of the universe? Of course not, so be diligent about *eliminating* this type of negativity from both your *thoughts* and *speech*. You should even work toward eliminating clichés like "this is killing me," or "this always happens to me."

It takes time and effort to systematically break old speech habits and develop new ones. Don't feel bad when you make mistakes. Whenever you catch yourself slipping into an old habit, stop and visualize yourself in the same circumstance, but saying the *right* thing. Keep working at this. The Bible itself, the very Word of God can be our greatest ally when we face difficult situations:

✠ *For the Word of God is **living** and **active.** **Sharper than any double-edged sword**... (Hebrews 4:12).*

To get an idea just how life-saving this weapon is, look at Jesus' response when He was confronted directly by satan, as recorded in Matthew 4:1-11. In this passage, we learn that Jesus quoted God's Word to satan in response to each of satan's temptations. There is power in God's Word. It would be wise for us to follow Jesus' lead and counter satan's advances and all of life's trials with the Word of God spoken in faith.

Speaking God's Word out loud has an additional benefit because:

...faith comes from hearing the message, and the message is heard through the Word of Christ (Romans 10:17).

You can build on your faith simply by listening to God's Word—from your own mouth, in your personal study, in community with others, during a church service or Sunday school. You can even take advantage of the Bible on CD, too, and fill your drive-time or anytime with an ipod listening to God's Word to help build up your faith. Remember the adage in computer programming: "Garbage in garbage out, good in good out."

ACTION & VISUALIZATION

Listen to and speak God's Word in your life, trusting in the Word's power to help you face difficult times.

YOUR VISION OR FORESIGHT

Foresight is seeing ahead of time where to go in life. If you want to run in life, not walk, crawl, or stand still, you need to have a clear vision of your desired future.

✠ *Where there is no vision, the people perish…*(Proverbs 29:18 KJV).

✠ *Then the Lord answered me and said: "Write the vision and make it plain on tablets, that he may run who reads it"* (Habakkuk 2:2 NKJV).

If you are walking through the woods but not sure where you're going, you have to move slowly and hesitantly to find your destination. However, if you have a clear vision of where you want to go, you can move quickly toward your goal. This is why I have inserted Visualization reminders throughout this book. It is my hope that when you encounter these, you put the book down, close your eyes, and visualize a specific change in your life as if you are actually acting it out.

Every so often it's good to visualize the things that have occurred as a result of your salvation and the changes you desire for the future. Also consider these things in your visualization: 1) how you *see* yourself as different; 2) how you will *act* differently than you did before when you find yourself in certain situations; and 3) how you imagine God fulfilling His promises to you, leading you to the fulfillment of His unique and special plan for your life.

Having a clear picture of your desired actions in situations retrains your internal programming to respond in kind, even subconsciously. Visualizing a desired outcome will help break mindless habits. Remember the Israelite spies who saw themselves as grasshoppers compared to the giants? They did not visualize themselves properly and they became how they visualized themselves: *insignificant*. What you see you will be!

Visualizing God's promises growing in your life will help line up your actions with your words, because you're then speaking what you are already seeing. Lining up your words, actions, thoughts, and heart is the key to having limitless faith. I'm not saying this is easy to do or that it will come quickly. You wouldn't expect a newborn baby to be able to run—the child needs to grow and then, through trial and error, discover the ability to first walk, then run.

What are you wishing or hoping for? Do you want to break an addiction? Restore a broken relationship? Find a new job? Visualize it. Dwell on it and confess it before God as you pray. Hope and confession are inexplicably tied together and can help encourage and build the other in crafting that unwavering faith required to move mountains. When you are successful at visualizing your future even when things get rough, you will see the promise of hope, power, and authority *no matter what* the circumstances.

✞ *So we fix our eyes not on what is seen, but on what is unseen. For what is seen is* **temporary,** *but what is unseen is* **eternal** (2 Corinthians 4:18).

ACTION & VISUALIZATION
*Have a clear vision of what you hope for
as well as who you are in Christ.*

ALIGN YOURSELF WITH GOD

God wants your actions and words to be congruent with your faith in Him. This puts you in sync with Him and allows the two of you to share a joyful and powerful life—*your life.* What happens when you're not in sync with God?

Suppose your spouse left town for a week. You would not actually *see* him or her for that week; however, to keep your relationship strong, wouldn't your spouse expect your actions to continue as if he or she were still at home? Even though you may be apart, you both would expect the love you have for each other to continue. And you would expect actions that backed this up, right? But, what if they didn't? What if either one of you decided "out of sight, out of mind" and chose to act single? Sound like a recipe for trouble? Absolutely!

Your relationship with God works in much the same way. Though you may speak to Him once in a while and perhaps listen even less—He still exists between those times. God still expects us to remember His love for us and our love for Him—this keeps the relationship *vibrant* and *real.* This also keeps us on the right path for our lives.

A real relationship with God demands that we line up our actions *each* day, not just when it seems convenient. Perhaps you know this scenario— it's Sunday morning and you're open and engaged to experience God in a very real way. You feel great—inspired, joyful, encouraged. It's almost as if you're "high" on God when you're worshiping Him at church. Your problems and circumstances seem to grow dimmer in His presence.

But then Monday comes. And Tuesday. And so on. The energy and excitement of shared worship or challenging teaching gives way to the stress of work and the demands of a busy life. Did God leave? Not at all. He's just as real and available on Wednesday morning in the middle of a work day as He is on Sunday morning when the music is lifting your spirit.

It takes a conscious awareness to develop an ongoing connection with God's presence—beyond a "church high." This is part of your faith maturation process—learning to feel and trust God's nearness when life seems to push Him far away. But He isn't far! In fact, God is right by your side at *all* times. Having faith in this fact will bring a better awareness of Him in your daily life. Look at what the apostle Paul says about mature faith:

✠ *No, in all things we are more than conquerors through Him who loved us. For I am **convinced** that neither death nor life, neither angels nor demons, neither height nor depth, nor anything else in all creation, will be able to separate us from the love of God that is in Christ Jesus our Lord* (Romans 8:37-39).

ACTION & VISUALIZATION

*Learn to trust in God's nearness and stay connected
with Him throughout each day.*

YOU HAVE ENOUGH FAITH

You might wonder at times if God gave you enough faith. Jesus' disciples certainly did, and on one occasion asked Jesus for more.

✠ *The apostles said to the Lord, "Increase our faith!" He replied, "If you have faith as small as a mustard seed, you can say to the mulberry tree, 'Be uprooted and planted in the sea,' and it will obey you"* (Luke 17:5-6).

Jesus responded that they didn't need any more because it takes only a very *small* amount of faith to do a *big job*.

LEVERAGE YOUR FAITH

Some may have faith in something that you do not have faith in or they may even have faith in the opposite. We have collectively been given dominion over the earth. You will recall reading in the previous chapter that Jesus Himself could not do many healings in the area where He grew up because the local people did not believe in Him as a healer. They saw Him as the son of a local carpenter so He could perform only a few miracles. Yet when He went across the sea where they saw Him as the Christ, He healed many. Their faith in His power and their desire to see Jesus manifest that power is what acted as a catalyst to release it.

You, too, will find times when the disbelief that is around you stifles your faith. And yet at other times, miracles will come easy when people who see Christ in you also believe in His limitless power. This is why it is important to leverage your faith with others of strong faith. And likewise you should avoid situations where other people's faith will work against yours.

Regularly when Jesus and His disciples were healing, they would remove disbelief from the area.

⊕
Peter went with them, and when he arrived he was taken upstairs to the room [where Tabitha, a disciple, lay dead]. *All the widows stood around him, crying and showing him the robes and other clothing that Dorcas had made while she was still with them. Peter sent them all out of the room; then he got down on is knees and prayed. Turning toward the dead woman, he said, "Tabitha get up." She opened her eyes, and seeing Peter she sat up* (Acts 9:39-40).

When there are people around you whose faith contradicts yours, in these times it is not always wise to let them know what you are believing for their faith will only rise up against yours. Likewise, you can use other people's faith to help you accomplish God's permissive will.

In Lystra there sat a man crippled in his feet, who was lame from birth and had never walked. He listened to Paul as he was speaking. Paul looked *directly at him, **saw that he had faith to be healed** and called out, "Stand up on your feet!" At that, the man jumped up and began to walk* (Acts 14:8-10).

This is why it is good to surround yourself with people of strong faith who are believing in what you are believing for so you can leverage off each others' faith. There is a synergy in faith which is why it's so *important for the church to become unified.*

ACTION & VISUALIZATION

Seek out others of strong faith who will support your faith.

FACING CIRCUMSTANCES WITH FAITH

Faith is dynamic—it's something we need to have 24/7. It's easy to have faith when things are going well. What about the things that challenge our faith? The prayers that go unanswered? The relationships that continue to go unhealed? What do we do when we hope for things and see nothing change? Do we desire and hope in vain?

Understanding what causes challenges to your faith will help you ready a faithful response when adversity comes. The following are some common hurdles—challenges to our faith:

- Sin in the world and in us.

- The enemy.

- Reaping what we sow.

- Loving discipline.

- God's purpose and perspective.

SIN IN THE WORLD AND IN US

As we have already discussed, we live in a fallen world. Sin entered the world because of free will and it reaches all the way to you and me. The Bible also states that even the earth itself is in travail or pain—perhaps the reason our world suffers from deadly hurricanes, tsunamis, and other such things. Daily we face the effects of that sin, whether because of the world's state of imperfection, or the free-will choices of other sinners. Did someone curse at you today? Cut you off in traffic? Ignore you? In these ways and many others, our faith is challenged by sin.

We also cause self-inflicted wounds when we sin. Maybe *you* were the person cursing someone out or cutting them off in traffic. These may seem like little things (and in the scheme of things, perhaps they are), but they are still examples of an imperfect heart and the power of free will to choose right or wrong in any given circumstance. When we sin, we undermine our faith. In fact, we toss it out the window, choosing not God's will but our own. The more our faith is built up, the less allure sin has in our lives— Jesus can then reign supreme.

The effects of sin are delayed, allowing us time to seek redemption, so when you do sin be quick to seek forgiveness and redemption.

YOU HAVE AN ENEMY

The Bible says you have an enemy in this world.

*Be self-controlled and alert. Your enemy, the devil, prowls around like a roaring lion looking for someone to devour. Resist him, standing firm in the **faith**, because you know that your brothers throughout the world are undergoing the same kind of sufferings* (1 Peter 5:8-9).

Clearly you have an enemy in this world who will bring challenges your way; however, your actions of faith give you the power to overcome him. I believe that says it all.

REAPING WHAT WE SOW

Simply put, what you dish out to others will be served back to you at some point. If you smile a lot and are a positive, giving person, then generally people will respond in a similar way. While many believe this on some level, it's surprising to see how often they act in ways that suggest otherwise. We can get so caught up in our own "stuff" that we forget everything we do affects those around us. Therefore, it cycles back around to affect us as well, both in a very direct obvious way and also in spiritual ways, which are often hard to see. As we learn to walk in faith, we plan positive and God-honoring attitudes and actions, knowing that what goes around comes around.

LOVING DISCIPLINE

✠ *...the Lord disciplines those He **loves**, as a father the son he delights in* (Proverbs 3:12).

There are several aspects to this concept of being disciplined that you need to understand so you can fully appreciate and recognize when you are being disciplined; but primarily we need to understand the word *loving*.

✠ *Love is patient, love is kind ...It is not rude, it is not self-seeking, it is not easily angered, it keeps no record of wrongs ...It always protects, always trusts, always hopes, always perseveres. Love never fails...* (1 Corinthians 13:4-8).

Since God *is* love, He only disciplines in love—patiently, kindly, not based on the past, not self-seeking, protectively, and so on. Though it is true our earthly parents sometimes discipline in this way, they may have also disciplined out of frustration, in anger, out of self interests, or they are (or were) just plain in the *wrong*.

Some people believe God disciplines by swatting us every time we get out of line. That's an interesting image, but *wrong*! One way God disciplines is with the invisible laws He set up to benefit, serve, and protect us. However, we must work within these invisible laws for them to have their intended effect.

Is physical pain a good thing? Pain hurts! Pain is created by the central nervous system God designed in you and does have a beneficial purpose. If you put your hand on a hot stove, without the shock of pain, would you move it? The pain caused by the hot burner may not feel good, but it is essential for your body's preservation. Pain alerts you that something is *wrong*.

God designed many systems (immune, nervous, digestive, thought, sight, hearing, emotions) and layers upon layers of physical laws and spiritual laws that work together for the good of His children. I imagine in the garden when the whole world was in perfect harmony, Adam and Eve never received sharp "painful" feedback. Now in this fallen world there are many things that can bring devastating harm and even death. So when you do something or expose yourself to something that could permanently damage you physically, psychologically, or spiritually, you will often encounter uncomfortable or now even painful events.

These are warnings to adjust behavior before we're badly damaged. Some people try and cover these uncomfortable feelings with painkillers like drugs, drinking alcohol to excess, or other behaviors intended to deflect or distract. Even the pursuit of happiness can be an attempt to avoid an uncomfortable or empty feeling. These are vain attempts to plug our ears so we can't hear God speaking to us.

God presents to us these spiritual laws through the Bible, through His Spirit and through everyday circumstances. Trial and error is a painful way to learn, and often needless since God allows "open Book" testing. That's one more reason why it is important to read the Bible and soak up all of God's truth so we can avoid some of those damaging and painful experiences. Out of this learning and trusting, we change our hearts, minds, actions—and our lives. Remember:

✠ *Keep your heart with **all** diligence, for out of it spring the issues of life* (Proverbs 4:23 NKJV).

Let's see what the author of Hebrews said about discipline.

✠ *And you have forgotten that word of encouragement that addresses you as sons: "**My son, do not make light of the Lord's discipline, and do not lose heart when He rebukes you, because the Lord disciplines those He loves, and He punishes everyone He accepts as a son.**" Endure hardship as discipline; God is treating you as sons. For what son is not disciplined by his father? If you are not disciplined (and everyone undergoes discipline), then you are illegitimate children and not true sons. Moreover, we have all had human fathers who disciplined us and we respected them for it. How much more should we submit to the Father of our spirits and live! Our fathers disciplined us for a little while as they thought best; but God disciplines us for **our good**, that we may **share in His holiness**. No discipline seems pleasant at the time, but painful. **Later on,** however, it* *produces a harvest of righteousness and peace for those **who have been trained by it*** (Hebrews 12:5-11).

God's discipline is for your benefit as it brings circumstances intended to adjust your behavior in ways that will allow you to live a more abundant life. God's discipline is *not* just to punish you for punishment's sake. God doesn't love us because we are perfect or even close. It is only through His perfect will and perfect timing that we can receive His gifts, finding long-term growth and restoration. Indeed God has circumvented our negative actions against Him to hardwire a system that points us back to restoration and eternal life—away from destruction and death. So when things take a turn from the outcome you hoped for, be open to what God may be saying. In fact seek the answer from Him alone, and eventually you will find it if you're patient, diligent, and remain open to hear His answer.

✞ *... seek and you will find...*(Matthew 7:7).

Remember, Jesus said of some people of His time.

✞ *...though seeing, they do not see; though hearing they do not hear or understand* (Matthew 13:13).

You will not want this said of you so it is important to *look* and *listen* carefully for God in *all* your circumstances so you can benefit from what He is saying to you.

Some of the trials and tribulations in life are like bumps in the road. Imagine driving with a coffee cup in your lap. When you hit a bump, what's *already in the cup splashes out*. It's these bumps in the road of life that allow us to see what's in us as well. When you're on "easy street" it's natural to have faith, praise God, be generous, and love others. But what comes out when we hit a bump in life? Does a confident, praising, and loving spirit over flow? Or does a fearful, retreating, complaining, and self-focused spirit splash out? It's common to put on a "Why me, God?" attitude when we hit those bumps. Don't feel condemned when this happens—none of us has been perfected yet. These bumps are actually part of the process of being perfected. They help *you* see what's *in you* or what you're *made of* so you can continue to *make adjustments*.

I want to reiterate that I am not saying God is designing *all* of the trials, tribulations, and suffering as a way to train you. Some things we bring on ourselves, some are correction from God, and some are attacks by satan. I *am* saying that no matter what created the bump, there is in *each* one a good gift God can use to improve us if we *choose* to see it and use it.

It may be difficult to fully appreciate this now, but there are things in you (habits, thoughts, and desires) that need to change before you can be conformed to the image and likeness of God. Some of these problems are deeply embedded in us and change will not come easily (or without pain). Adversity can be a purifying process intended to filter bad habits, thoughts, and desires—sin—to refine a new kind of purity in you.

✠ *Therefore this is what the Lord Almighty says: "See, I will refine and test them, for what else can I do because of the sin of My people?"* (Jeremiah 9:7)

✠ *But He knows the way that I take; when He has tested me, I will come forth as gold* (Job 23:10).

The only way to get impurities out of gold and silver is to heat them up to a very, very high temperature so that the impurities float to the top and are burned away. Physically we are designed in the same way. When we are infected with a bacteria that is not good for us, our bodies naturally rise to a higher temperature (a fever) to help us kill that infection so we can be healthy and purified again. The same idea of a refining process seems to be true as it relates to our character and spirit. Sometimes it takes a very, very high heat to burn away those things embedded deep in our hearts.

✠ *The crucible for silver and the furnace for gold, but the Lord tests the heart* (Proverbs 17:3).

When the heat comes, and it will, you will want to remember:

✠ *Blessed is the man whom God corrects; so do not despise the discipline of the Almighty* (Job 5:17).

✠ *Blessed is the man who perseveres under trial, because when he has stood the test, he will receive the crown of life that God has promised to those who love Him* (James 1:12).

✠ *Whoever loves discipline loves knowledge, but he who hates correction is stupid* (Proverbs 12:1).

✠ *He who scorns instruction will pay for it, but he who respects a command is rewarded* (Proverbs 13:13).

✠ *He who ignores discipline despises himself, but whoever heeds correction gains understanding* (Proverbs 15:32).

ACTION & VISUALIZATION

Expect and accept discipline willingly and thankfully.

GOD'S PURPOSE AND PERSPECTIVE

Sometimes things happen in your life that may simply be part of God's greater plan. Although you may not understand these things now, they have a purpose. Sometimes that purpose looks like a delay, another detour away from our hope. However, though seemingly late to us God's time is always perfect.

✠ *For the revelation awaits an appointed time...though it lingers, wait for it; it will certainly come and will not delay* [past God's appointed time] (Habakkuk 2:3).

Consider this story from the Book of Acts:

✠ *One day Peter and John were going up to the temple at the time of prayer—at three in the afternoon. Now a man crippled from birth was being carried to the temple gate called Beautiful, where he was put **every day** to beg from those going into the temple courts. When he saw Peter and John about to enter, he asked them for money. Peter looked straight at him, as did John. Then Peter said, "Look at us!" So the man gave them his attention, expecting to get something from them. Then Peter said, "Silver or gold I do not have, but what I have I give you. In the name of Jesus Christ of Nazareth, walk." Taking him by the right hand, he helped him up, and instantly the man's feet and ankles became strong. He jumped to his feet and began to walk. Then he went with them into the temple courts, walking and jumping, and praising God. When all the people saw him walking and praising*

God, they recognized him as the same man who used to sit begging at the temple gate called Beautiful, and they were filled with wonder and amazement at what had happened to him (Act 3:1-10).

The lame man sat at the entrance of the gate called Beautiful every day. People knew him—even Jesus Himself would have passed this man, as we know He went through this gate. But for some reason, Jesus did not choose to heal him when He Himself passed by. Instead, in God's time and for God's purpose, Peter and John were called upon to heal the lame man in the name of Jesus, and in front of a large crowd. The account goes on to say that Peter started preaching to the crowd of people who were suddenly intrigued because of the miracle. Here was the ultimate result of the delay in the blind man's healing:

But many who heard the message believed, and the number of men grew to about five thousand (Acts 4:4).

From a worldly perspective, it may seem odd that Jesus didn't heal this man much earlier. Perhaps it's even a bit perplexing that God would allow him to be lame in the first place. However, look at this story from a larger spiritual perspective and see how the lame man could be part of God's plan and purpose of bringing him and others to Himself. Let's take a look at another story—this one of a man who has been blind from birth—whom Jesus and His disciples encounter. Jesus' disciples ask Him who sinned—who caused the man's blindness—the blind man or his parents? Read His answer from the Gospel of John:

*"Neither this man nor his parents sinned," said Jesus, "but this happened so that **the work of God might be displayed in his life**"* (John 9:3).

When the blind man received salvation and sight from God's "display in his life," his neighbors and those who observed the healing spread the word of the miracle until it even caught the attention of the Pharisees, who were leading the people astray from God. As a result of this circumstance, Jesus was able to teach an important spiritual lesson to the blind man and countless others that had eternal consequences of life and death for them.

How would you feel if you knew your blindness or other infirmity was for the very purpose of giving God the opportunity to reveal Himself to you and to others? Or perhaps so you could have a closer and more intimate relationship with Him? These are very difficult questions to wrestle with. They force us to admit that some spiritual things are simply beyond our natural mind's understanding. We can't fully comprehend how secondary in importance this life we live on earth is, compared to the eternal life that follows. How minor the physical things in life are compared to the spiritual truths God seeks to teach us.

Yes, God could heal everyone in the blink of an eye. He could stop all alcoholics from craving liquor and mend every broken marriage. Yet He doesn't always correct the things we have brought upon ourselves. Instead He uses every adversity, sickness, addiction, accident, and challenging relationship to draw us and others closer to Him. Is it more important for us to have complete comfort in this temporal life without developing a relationship with God, or is developing a very internal relationship with our Creator the most important thing? God didn't create, nor does He want, battery-powered robot believers. He wants you, out of your own free will, to grow close to Him and be like Him because that is why He created you. This is important for you because ultimately it is where you find your true source of sustenance, joy, life, and fulfillment.

✝ *Woe to him who quarrels with his Maker, to him who is but a potsherd among the potsherds on the ground. Does the clay say to the potter, "What are you making?" Does your work say, "He has no hands?"* (Isaiah 45:9)

God is playing out a great plan for the world that involves billions of souls. There is interplay between God and satan, good and evil as it relates to our will both individually and corporately which we can not fully appreciate. Consider Job, whom the Bible indicates was a righteous man. Job became involved in a high stakes contest where it was ultimately proven to satan that Job did not love God *merely because* God gave him many earthly things and good health. Job was faithful, even when he was stripped of his family, money, career, and left alone, homeless, covered in boils and body sores. The question that comes to each of us is: "Could I do the same?"

And yet we learn in the Book of Job that Job's faith was *strengthened* because of and through this initially *devastating* process. Job also developed a deeper understanding of God and a more intimate relationship with Him. Are you willing to give up some comfort and even possessions for a deeper understanding and closer relationship with God? In the Old Testament story of Job it says God spoke to him in the midst of his troubles. It is often in the midst of your troubles when God is most likely to speak to you. There is a saying that God whispers in your pleasure, speaks in your conscience, but shouts in your pain. Sometimes hardship gives God the opportunity to teach you significant things. In the face of adversity, in the height of the storm, look at Job's understanding and faith in his ultimate destiny with God:

✝ *I know that my Redeemer lives, and that in the end He will stand upon earth. And after my skin has been destroyed yet in my flesh I will see God; I myself will see Him with my own eyes—I, and not another. How my heart yearns within me!* (Job 19:25-27)

In the midst of Job's troubles, God was speaking—helping him know that in "the end" he would receive in the resurrection a new body by which he would see God. God is always speaking to us, but in the midst of our biggest troubles we simply are more open to hearing His voice.

☦ *For God does speak—now one way, now another—though men may not percieve it* (Job 33:14).

Through these troubles, Job and God brought their relationship to a *higher level.* After Job had fully unwrapped the trials and tribulations, for all of his suffering, he was physically rewarded *double* the possessions he started with. Job accepted God's will for his life, stayed on God's path, and found his reward. You too will have trials that, if handled properly, will allow you to see God and receive your reward.

☦ *...though now for a little while you may have had to suffer grief in all kinds of trials. These have come so that your faith—of greater worth than gold, which perishes even though refined by fire—may be proved genuine and may result in praise, glory and honor when Jesus Christ is revealed. Though you have not seen Him, you love Him; and even though you do not see Him now, you believe in Him and are filled with an inexpressible and glorious joy, for you are receiving the goal of your faith, the salvation of your souls* (1 Peter 1:6-9).

God has a purpose for everything and plans to work everything out for the good of those He loves. We just don't always understand how or why—or God's perfect timing. Remember that God moves according to a timetable we can't comprehend. While we may sometimes think He is being slow to respond, it may be that we're simply not ready to hear an answer—or the particular answer God is giving. Our calling at these times is to just stay on His path even if we don't understand where it is going at the time.

ACTION & VISUALIZATION

See God's hand in both good and bad circumstances;
align your heart and actions with God's purpose.

If you have felt confined by life, with habits, thoughts, and actions you can't seem to break out of, take heart! Remember the caterpillar and the struggle from cocoon to flight. Let this struggle lead you to receive, unwrap, and use the Gifts of Freedom He offers. They will give you the freedom and spiritual wings that allow you to fly.

...We were under great pressure, far beyond our ability to endure, so that we despaired even of life. Indeed, in our hearts we felt the sentence of death. But this happened that we might not rely on ourselves but on God, Who raises the dead. He has delivered us from such a deadly peril, and He will deliver us. On Him we have set our hope [with actions of faith] *that He will continue to deliver us...*(2 Corinthians 1:8-10).

In summary, acting in faith—even a strong faith—won't eliminate problems in your life *nor* will it trump God's will. However, acting in faith *will* allow you to overcome adversities and discover joy along the way. Most importantly, using your gift of faith by putting it into action opens His heart so you can enjoy intimacy between you and your Maker.

MEDITATION POINT

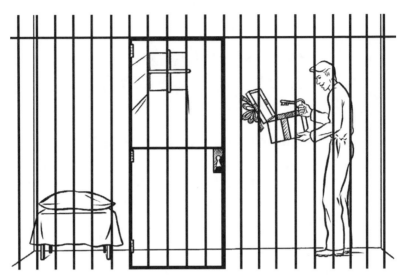

Put your faith in opening the gifts and He will give you a spiritual way out-sometimes physical, too.

Go to Chapter 7 in the Study Guide section on page 305.

Chapter 8

GIFT #4—ADVERSITY

HOW CAN FAITH TURN ADVERSITY INTO VICTORY?

Before you begin to read, pray that the Holy Spirit
will give you understanding and application.

✝ *Even though I walk through the valley of the shadow of death, I will
fear no evil, for You are with me; Your rod and Your staff, they comfort me* (Psalm 23:4).

Walt Disney was turned down 302 times before he got financing
for the "happiest place on earth." Colonel Sanders spent two
years driving across the country with chicken recipes, which
were turned down 1,009 times. Thomas Edison failed 10,000 times before
he succeeded in creating the electric light. David was homeless and running for his life when he wrote Psalm 23:4 (above). He went on to become
the most powerful king in the world.

So what's the point? You must let your faith drive you through the valleys of life while at the same time receiving the *gift* each adversity you
encounter has to offer. Inventors use adversity and setbacks as a process to
refine their products. They don't give up. Instead they take from each adversity what they can and move on in faith toward their goal. In a spiritual

sense, David, like Job, used adversity in his life to build up his faith and strengthen his relationship with God.

Reread the opening verse to make sure you comprehend how strong David's relationship with God had grown. So much so that he gained comfort by feeling God's loving and protective presence around him in times of terror. Isn't this a place you would like to be—a place where you can be fearless in the face of adversity? This does not come magically, but with experience and exercise gained through our adversities in life.

I am not saying that adversity is itself a gift or good. However, the existence of adversity in our lives produces gifts—gifts born out of adversity. Remember,

✝ *... we know that in **all** things God works for the good of those who love Him, who have been called according to His purpose* (Romans 8:28).

As believers, we can have the same confidence as David did that God ties redemption, resurrection power, and adversity together—no matter how or why the adversity came about. God uses adversity to usher in the gifts He gives us. Adversity was the unfortunate result of God giving humankind the freedom of choice. Although the choice in the Garden disconnected us from our intimate relationship with God, He restored this relationship through Jesus and set us back onto His original course. To bring us closer He imbeds redemptive gifts in the adversity we ourselves have brought about. It is important to be open to these gifts and use them.

After reading the two previous chapters about faith, you can probably see many of the different gifts found within adversity.

- Without adversity and challenges, you would have no victory.

- Without loss and failure, you would have no redemption.

- Without adversity and resistance, you could not grow and develop strength.

- Without adversity and trials, you could not refine your character.

- Without adversity, great testimonies could not be created to lead others to Jesus.

- Without adversity, how would we know our daily need for God?

Indeed, the biggest gift found within adversity is that it drives us *closer to God*. And that closeness allows us to take our eyes off the physical present, the earthly here and now, to envision something much greater—our eternal future with Him.

David recognized he was only passing "through" a valley; it wasn't a permanent home because he knew and believed in a promise from the Creator of the universe that he would eventually rest in a better place. Our foresight, our faith, doesn't rest in the physical—in selling millions of chicken wings or tickets to an amusement park. Our foresight, our faith, rests in Christ's statement, "I go to prepare a place for you"—a place beyond our imagination. And this is the kind of vision, the only kind of faith that can see you through life's *darkest, deepest valleys* like David experienced.

Painful lows and struggles here on earth should also remind us that this world is not our permanent home; Jesus wants to comfort us in this truth:

[Jesus said] *"Do not let your hearts be troubled. Trust in God; trust also in Me. In My Father's house are many rooms; if it were not so, I would have told you. I am going there to prepare a place for you. And if I go and prepare a place for you, I will come back and take you to be with Me that you also may be where I am"* (John 14:1-3).

Don't forget that God's original intent was for us to live in the Garden of Eden here on earth, not the valley of the shadow of death. Our choices and the natural consequences of sin have led us through the valleys. Through His resurrection power our final destination will be like the Garden—a place where we live in God's presence and enjoy the splendor He intended for us—a place without the adversities we now face in life. In this place, the City of God:

✠ *There will be no more night. They [you] will not need the light of a lamp or the light of the sun, for the Lord God will give them light...* (Revelation 22:5).

Imagine it—you'll be remade in God's image and likeness, experiencing the fullness of His love with no distortion of sin—in harmony with all that is around you. And God's presence will be enough to provide you with light!

But because of sin we brought on ourselves, we have work to do before we get to this glorious city; however, the very adversities we run into while getting there have gifts inside to better equip and prepare us. The question remains: will you choose to unwrap all the gifts God gives you—even those found within adversity? Your proper handling of adversity can be a powerful witness of God's love, and a vehicle to bring life to a dying world.

KEEP A GOOD PERSPECTIVE

If your exercise coach told you he was giving you a free exercise machine to use at home, you'd probably feel pretty good about that. However, to use this gift to its full benefit, you'd have to work out, sweat, and train, perhaps experiencing some pain. Likewise, we should be joyful when trials and adversity come our way because they give us a chance to exercise our faith. In essence, adversity is your exercise machine and you can't build up your faith and/or refine yourself without it. There is no way to build up your muscles without resistance; it takes resistance or adversity to build up your faith. You also need to stretch your muscles *regularly* to retain full range and use of them—faith is the same. We must have the proper knowledge and perspective to get the most out of opportunities life offers.

Sometimes when we fail at reaching one of our goals or have challenges or adversity in life, we feel as if we are out of God's will and nothing good is happening. However, consider this story about a man's faith. God asked the man to push a large rock. In faith, the man obediently started pushing the rock with all his strength, yet it would not move. The man had such a high level of faith that he went out every day diligently pushing on the rock for an hour. After a month of seeing no movement he decided to also start studying the Bible to see if he could find people in similar situation and learn how they dealt with it. After another month of pushing on the rock and reading the Bible every day, yet seeing no movement in the rock, the man started talking to God about it daily. He continued to see no movement.

He questioned God: "Is it me?" "Are there changes in my life I need to make to complete Your will?" "Why am I failing to move the rock?" After a month of dialogue with God, God said to the man, "I asked you to push the rock, *not move it*. By obediently pushing it, you moved yourself into a better position." In his faithful efforts of pushing on the rock, the man improved his physical strength, his mental knowledge of the Bible, and intimacy with God. While the man thought he was loosing, he was really winning!

God has also given you a rock to push. You live on it—*earth*. By pushing on this rock to move it His way, though you may not always be successful at your goal, you will *certainly* be successful in building yourself up into a better person by faithfully pushing on the world in which you live.

Along with the gift of faith, God gives us a promise to help us *embrace* the adversities of life. Romans 8:28 gives us this perspective: "all things are working together for our good." Therefore, it is up to us to use faith and act on this promise. God wants us to be joyful, an enduring state that abides with us, unlike happiness. Remember this discussion in Chapter 3?

You start growing your strength, confidence, and joy from the *inside*, not the outside. When seemingly bad things happen, you should *not* be driven to a place of fear and defeat; instead have confidence in God's love and resurrection power. Out of this response we are positioned to see the gifts imbedded in adversity. From this vantage point, adversities become testimonies of God's power, blessings, and growth.

This is an important point to grasp. We as Christians are designed to work from the inside out and not the outside in. Our joy and peace should *not* come from the physical world, because when we were saved, the real world, the world that matters was created in us that day.

✟ *Once, having been asked by the Pharisees when the kingdom of God would come, Jesus replied, "The Kingdom of God does not come with your careful observation, nor will people say, 'Here it is,' or 'There it is,' because* **the Kingdom of God is within you***"* (Luke 17:20-21).

You will learn and experience God through prayer, worship, praise, spiritual achievements, and even adversity. Your experiences with God can give you an inner peace that allows you to receive the joy God desires for you.

✟ *Do not fear, little flock, for it is your Father's good pleasure to give you the Kingdom* (Luke 12:32 NKJV).

If you have faith in God and trust that God can use your adversity for good—physical, mental or spiritual—then you will know that your trials and sufferings are only temporary. Trusting God now, before, during, and after your troubles provides you with supernatural joy. Even in the hardest times, blue skies will open up within you when you unwrap all His Gifts.

Let's recap. Why is having a strong faith important? Faith in action shows our belief in God, both His promises and His nature. Faith in action helps us get through difficult times, holding onto God's promises and nature. And most importantly, faith pleases God and brings us closer to Him. So how is your faith built up and exercised? Through adversity.

Don't Give Up

Beyond the joy, we need to believe that trials and adversity will result in something to help us achieve our purpose. When you graduated from school, your goal may have been to run a company. However, without first having the trials and challenges of actual business experience, you are likely to fail. We need personal experience to develop the skill and talent we need to reach our goals. This applies to our spiritual development as well. God is building into you the tools, friendships, and character you need to become what He wants you to be. A reminder: "All things God works for the good of those who love Him."

Don't let adversity rattle your faith—don't give up before you get *through* the valley to where God desires you to be. Some people lose faith in the face of an adversity and turn an opportunity for victory into defeat. They pitch their tent in the valley or even start building their house there. When trouble is surrounding you, I believe in following this old adage: "If you find yourself going through hell…don't stop, keep going!" You need to understand things in this temporal world are subject to change. Tomorrow is another day.

…weeping may remain for a night, but rejoicing comes in the morning (Psalms 30:5).

The Old Testament is filled with stories about people who kept moving through the valleys and they saw their faith and relationships continually increase as they moved through to the other side. One of the most familiar stories is David and Goliath. David's story begins when he was merely a shepherd boy. The destiny God was shaping for David to become the king of Israel brought him through a truly monumental valley—a confrontation with a warrior named Goliath:

✠ *A champion named Goliath, who was from Gath, came out of the Philistine camp. He was over **nine feet** tall. He had a bronze helmet on his head and wore a coat of scale **armor** of bronze weighing five thousand shekels [about 125 pounds]; on his legs he wore bronze greaves, and a bronze javelin was slung on his back. His spear shaft was like a weaver's rod, and its **iron point** weighed six hundred shekels [about 15 pounds]. His shield bearer went ahead of him. Goliath stood and shouted to the ranks of Israel, "Why do you come out and line up for battle? Am I not a Philistine, and are you not the servants of Saul? Choose a man and have him come down to me. If he is able to fight and kill me, we will become your subjects; but if I overcome him and kill him, you will become our subjects and serve us." Then the Philistine said, "This day I defy the ranks of Israel! Give me a man and let us fight each other." On hearing the Philistine's words, Saul and all the Israelites were **dismayed** and **terrified** (1 Samuel 17:4-11).*

David would probably have been too terrified to fight this 9-foot giant had it not been for the way God prepared him through *other challenges* they overcame together. See how David used them to build up his faith and confidence in God.

✠ *Saul replied [to David's request to be the one to fight Goliath], "You are not able to go out against this Philistine and fight him; you are only a boy, and he has been a fighting man from his youth." But David said to Saul, "Your servant has been keeping his father's sheep. When a **lion** or a **bear** came and carried off a sheep from the flock, I went after it, struck* *it and rescued the sheep from its mouth. When it turned on me, I seized it by its hair, struck it and killed it. Your servant has killed both the **lion** and the **bear**, this uncircumcised Philistine will be **like one of them**, because he has defied the armies of the living God* (1 Samuel 17:33-36).

David overcame a lion and a bear, as God was building his faith to handle the giant. These attacks by the lion and bear certainly would have seemed like problems at the time, but in reality they were building up his faith, his trust in God. What seemed bad at the time was actually preparing David so he would not give up when a much bigger challenge or adversity came into his life. Because David did not give up or run from these previous battles, he was prepared to fulfill the will of God—to defeat the *giant* in his life, and the one seeking to enslave his nation of Israel.

Each of David's prior adversities led to victory and created trust and depth in his relationship with God. Each adversity created a *compelling* testimony to help others build up their faith in God. Do you believe your actions of faith in the face of adversity will do the same? The only difference between David and the other Israelites is that David acted on the faith he was given and the others didn't. And just like David you can choose to act in faith daily—building up your strength to conquer your own giants.

Creating Testimonies

There is no question that you will face adversity. There may be attacks on you, your family, and your possessions. Perhaps you are experiencing some of these right now. Are you facing your own "lions" and "bears"—perhaps preparing you for an even greater challenge?

If you are in *sync* with God's will, then it is by faith that you can attack and defeat these lions, bears, and eventually, giants. In the physical realm, you may not see a way to defeat them; however, as you receive God's supernatural Gifts of Freedom, then, like David, you will find a supernatural *victory*. Instead of running away or giving up, you can find joy and strength in overcoming these circumstances. It says David *ran quickly* at Goliath when they fought. *Over time* David built up a fearless faith allowing him to say:

✝ *I will not fear the tens of thousands drawn up against me on every side* (Psalm 3:6).

It may be a long journey for you to get to this level of faith—but this is what God desires. This may even seem impossible today, but keep in mind that God doesn't give us things that are too difficult for us to handle.

✝ *No temptation had seized you except what is common to man. And God is faithful; He will not let you be tempted beyond what you can bear. But when you are tempted, He will also provide a way out so that you can stand up under it* (1 Corinthians 10:13).

God puts a gift in adversity so that we can have a way out *if we choose*. Not in our strength, but in His. This is where we find confidence.

✝ *...Be strong and courageous. Do not be terrified; do not be discouraged, for the Lord your God will be with you wherever you go* (Joshua 1:9).

✝ *For God did not give us a spirit of timidity, but a spirit of power, of love and of self-discipline* (2 Timothy 1:7).

✝ *... in all things we are more than conquerors through him who loves us* (Romans 8:37).

We will have setbacks and adversities because of the choices we have made, sins we've committed, and because the world in which we live is populated with fallen people doing evil—doing things not in the will of God. We will be knocked down, but not defeated. Be confident in this.

✠ *Do not gloat over me, my enemy! Though I have fallen, I will rise. Though I sit in darkness, the Lord will be my light. Because I have sinned against Him, I will bear the Lord's wrath, until He pleads my case and establishes my right. He will bring me out into the light; I will see His righteousness. Then my enemy will see it and will be covered with shame, she who said to me, "Where is the Lord your God?" My eyes will see her downfall; even now she will be trampled underfoot like mire in the streets* (Micah 7:8-10).

✠ *We are hard pressed on every side, but not crushed; perplexed, but not in despair; persecuted, but not abandoned; struck down, but not destroyed* (2 Corinthians 4:8-9).

So how do we turn our defeat into victory? Well, it is important to be open to God's leading because many of the biggest victories will *not* occur how and when our natural minds might expect. Remember the Israelites at Jericho? They were led by God to do something very unusual—walk around the walls and shout for seven days to receive their victory. Your spiritual solution to the physical battles you face may be hidden from your natural mind. When problems, battles, and adversities arise, look for and be open to the supernatural. Don't automatically assume and rely on conventional thinking. Remember, God's primary objective is for you to express your faith while at the same time creating a testimony for others to see. His ways are higher than ours—don't rule out God's often unorthodox approach to overcoming adversity.

Before David—a shepherd boy—fought Goliath, Saul offered David his own armor and weapons. While this would have been the traditional method of preparing for battle, David refused Saul's armor because of the way God had trained him. David instead armed himself in a very surprising and unnatural way:

✠ *Then he took his staff in his hand, chose five smooth stones from the stream, put them in the pouch of his shepherd's bag, and with his slings in hand, approached the Philistine...He [Goliath] looked David over and saw that he was only a boy, ruddy and handsome, and he despised him. He said to David, "Am I a dog that you come at me with sticks?" And the Philistine cursed David by his gods. "Come here," he said, "and I'll give your flesh to the birds of the air and the beasts of the field!" David said to the Philistine, "You come against me with sword and spear and javelin, but I come against you in the name of the Lord Almighty [in His will], the God of the armies of Israel, Whom you have defied. This day the Lord will hand you over to me, and I'll strike you down and cut off your head. Today I will give the carcasses of the Philistine army to the birds of the air and the beasts of the earth, and the whole world will know that there is a God in Israel. All those gathered here will know that it is not by sword or spear that the Lord saves; for the battle is the Lord's, and He will give all of you into our hands." As the Philistine moved closer to attack him, David ran quickly toward the battle line to meet him. Reaching into his bag and taking out a stone, he slung it and it struck the Philistine on the forehead. The stone sank into his forehead, and he fell facedown on the ground* (1 Samuel 17:40-49).

David then used Goliath's own sword to kill him and cut off his head. On seeing their hero killed, the other Philistines ran and were therefore easily defeated by the Israelites. They ran because they put their faith in a man— allbeit a man who was over 9 feet tall. Today we still have the tendency to idolize people of great strength, beauty, talent, speech, etc. When they fall their followers will also be scattered like Goliath's. In your walk of faith this is why it's important to stay focused on Jesus and not a head pastor or minister regardless of their seemingly great spiritual strength.

David was focused on God and only God. This strong faith David exhibited in God's will for him created a *testimony* to the world that God did indeed exist and was with David and the Israelites. God wants to build testimonies with you that reflect God's strength in you, giving you victory over your "giants." Your testimony, just as David's was, will be a light in a dying world for others that they may see God, too.

Some of what I have written here is in contradiction to a popular notion among many Christians that after we're saved, life should be smooth sailing. After all, as some Christians say, "God gives us the victory!" This statement is certainly true; however, what many Christians miss is that without a battle, how can there be a victory? Battles exist because there is an enemy of God, a force opposed to obedience to the will of God. Your faith in the battles gives you victory. Therefore, start developing a warrior's spirit—like David. Warriors carry shields to help defend themselves in battle. The Bible says *faith* is our *shield*—it's the one David used in his battle against the giant.

✝ *...take up the shield of faith, with which you can extinguish all the flaming arrows of the evil one* (Ephesians 6:16).

Did you catch that? The enemy isn't just shooting arrows at you—these are *flaming* arrows. It is up to you, with God's help, to raise your shield of faith and defend yourself when adversity comes.

✝ *...If you do not stand firm in your faith, you will not stand at all* (Isaiah 7:9).

<hr>

ACTION & VISUALIZATION

Stand strong in your faith when the inevitable attacks come,
and thereby create a testimony with God.

YOU ARE HIS GLORY ON EARTH

You live in a fallen world with an enemy who wants to bring you down. Jesus left you here as His occupation force for at least one specific purpose: to *show* the world God's love. Jesus Himself prayed this prayer to His Father:

✠ *My prayer is not that You take them* [believers] *out of the world but that You protect them from the evil one. They are not of the world, even as I am not of it. Sanctify them by the truth; Your word is truth...My prayer is... That all of them* [believers] *may be one, Father, just as You are in Me and I am in You. May they also be in Us so that the world may believe that You sent Me.* **I have given them the glory that You gave Me,** *that they may be one as We are One: I in them and You in Me. May they be brought to* **complete unity to let the world know that You sent Me** *and have loved them even as You have loved Me* (John 17:15-23).

When the world and your enemy take shots at you, will you follow David's example? Will you choose the road of faith in the face of fear? Will you choose to show the world God's love, resurrection power, and His glory in you? Truly, this is your mission as a Christian in this world. What's the point if our lives do not reflect the glory of God? Moses points this out to God:

✠ *Then Moses said to Him,* **"If your Presence does not go with us,** *do not send us up from here. How will anyone know that You are pleased with me and with Your people unless you go with us? What else will* *distinguish me and Your people from all the other people on the face of the earth?* (Exodus 33:15-16)

In our case as born-again believers, we all have God's presence *in us*; however, the world cannot see it unless *we act* in faith to show it to them. This is another reason why your action of faith pleases God—it shines His light into a dying world. It brings others closer to Him. We will have struggles as believers, but it is those very struggles that allows us to show God's presence in us and distinguishes us from the *other people*. When these challenges come, we can choose to either be a victim or a person who will built up our faith to glorify God in the world.

BE AN EXAMPLE

The more you exercise your faith, the closer you grow to God. You may have heard people refer to this relationship as "walking with God." Walking is an action, an exercise, a forward movement. That's why we don't ask, "How's your nap with God?" Faith in action is a catalyst for intimacy with Him. Enoch is an example of someone who walked closely with God.

Enoch walked with God; then he was no more; because God took him away (Genesis 5:24).

The phrase "walking with someone" denotes a constant and familiar interaction. This is the kind of relationship God desires us to have with him, a *oneness* where the *end* of Him and the *beginning* of us is hard to discern. The Hebrew word for *took* in this verse is *laqach* (law-kakh) which means "to get," "lay hold of," "snatch away," or "marry" as in take a wife. The image you should get from this verse is that Enoch walked so closely and in alignment with God that God enveloped him—they became *one* as in the marriage of a husband and wife. *Intimacy* with your Creator also leads us to *joy in adversity* that *others will notice* because it is completely contradictory to the world's standards—it's supernatural! The apostle Paul wrote about it this way:

✠ *We are hard pressed on every side, but not crushed; perplexed, but not in despair; persecuted, but not abandoned; struck down, but not destroyed. We always carry around in our body the death of Jesus, so that the life of Jesus may also be revealed in our body. For we who are alive are always being given over to death for Jesus' sake, so that His life may be revealed in our mortal body. So then, death is at work in us, but life is at work in you. It is written: "I believed; therefore I have spoken." With that same spirit of faith we also believe and therefore speak, because we know that the One who raised the Lord Jesus from the dead will also raise us with Jesus and present us with you in His presence. All this is for your benefit, so that the grace that is reaching more and more people may cause thanksgiving to overflow to the glory of God. Therefore we do not lose heart. Though outwardly we are wasting away, yet inwardly [spiritually] we are being renewed day by day. For our light and momentary troubles are achieving for us an eternal glory that far outweighs them all. So we fix our eyes not on what is seen, but on what is unseen. For what is seen is temporary, but what is unseen is eternal* (2 Corinthian 4:8-18).

All circumstances can help us build better spiritual muscles. Believers who have successfully built up faith through trials are a *powerful testimony* to young believers and non-believers alike. Their spiritual muscles are beautiful in the sight of God. God can do great works *in* you and *through* you when *you choose* to become the person He wants you to be.

✠ [Jesus said] *"...let your light shine before men..."* (Matthew 5:16).

We are warned that for some, the stakes will be high.

✠ [Jesus said] *"Do not be afraid of what you are about to suffer. I tell you, the devil will put some of you in prison to test you, and you will suffer persecution for ten days. Be faithful, even to the point of death, and I will give you the crown of life"* (Revelation 2:10).

ACTION & VISUALIZATION

Shine your light for others to see by exercising faith in adversity.

DON'T LOOK AT YOUR CIRCUMSTANCE

When you have a word from God, keep your faith in it regardless of your circumstances.

✠ *During the fourth watch of the night Jesus went out to them* [the disciples in a boat], *walking on the lake. When the disciples saw Him walking on the lake, they were terrified. "It's a ghost," they said, and cried out in fear. But Jesus immediately said to them: "Take courage! It is I. Don't be afraid." "Lord, if it's You," Peter replied, "tell me to come to You on the water." "**Come**," He said. Then Peter got down out of the boat, **walked on the water** and came toward Jesus* (Matthew 14:25-29).

Peter gets his word and in stepping out of the boat in faith he achieves a miracle…

✟ *But when he [Peter] saw the **wind** [his current circumstances] he was **afraid** and beginning to sink and cried out, "Lord, save me!" Immediately Jesus reached out His hand and caught him. "You have little faith," He said, "Why did you doubt?"* (Matthew 14:30-31)

Peter initially had faith in the word he received; but when he saw his circumstances, he became fearful, and fear is the opposite of faith so he lost his miracle. Though Peter did not hold onto his word from Jesus to keep from sinking, Jesus still held onto Peter so he wouldn't be overcome by the world's circumstances. Jesus' last words are important ones to ask yourself when you get caught up in your circumstances, "Why did you doubt?"

ACTION & VISUALIZATION

Look beyond your circumstances to keep God's Word in sight.

AN ASTOUNDING FAITH

Though it's impossible to assign a measurable value to faith or to rank biblical heroes according to their level of faith, I would be remiss if I didn't examine the life of the man who is often referred to as the "father of our faith"—Abraham. Abraham received a promise from God:

✟ *Then the Lord said, "I will surely return to you about this time next year, and Sarah your wife will have a son." Now Sarah was listening at the entrance to the tent, which was behind him. Abraham and Sarah were already old and well advanced in years, and Sarah was past the age of childbearing. So Sarah laughed to herself as she thought, "After I am worn out and my master is old, will I now have this pleasure?" Then the Lord said to Abraham, "Why did Sarah*

laugh and say, 'Will I really have a child, now that I am old?' Is any-
thing too hard for the Lord? I will return to you at the appointed time
next year and Sarah will have a son" (Genesis 18:10-14).

Despite the fact Sarah had never been able to have a child and now was
too old, God gave Abraham a promise that he would have a son with her
and Abraham's faith did not fail:

Against all hope, Abraham in hope believed and so became the father
of many nations, just as it had been said to him, "So shall your off-
spring be." Without weakening in his faith, he faced the fact that his
body was as good as dead—since he was about a hundred years old—
and that Sarah's womb was also dead. Yet he did not waver through
unbelief regarding the promise of God, but was strengthened in his
faith and gave glory to God, being fully persuaded that God had
power to do what He had promised. This is why "it was credited to
him as righteousness" (Romans 4:18-22).

Abraham's faith was accounted to him as righteousness. The word
accounted, *logidzomai* (log-id-zom-ahee) refers numerically to "adding up"
or metaphorically to the concept of drawing a conclusion. The idea here is
that when God added up the sum total of Abraham's life, he was considered
righteous *not* because he was perfect, but because of his faithful belief that
God would forgive him. Abraham didn't *earn* righteousness; he simply
received the gift of righteousness because of his great *actions* of faith in God[1].

Abraham, who was originally called Abram, followed God from the
beginning of his life.

The Lord had said to Abram, "Leave your country, your people and your
father's household and go to the land I will show you. I will make you

into a great nation and I will bless you; I will make your name great, and you will be a blessing. I will bless those who bless you, and whoever curses you I will curse; and all people on earth will be blessed through you." So Abram left, as the Lord had told him...(Genesis 12:1-4).

When God called Abraham to leave his country, his people, and his family—*he left.* This was a big step of faith. Can you imagine? Abraham had never seen God face to face, yet he trusted Him. Look at how Abraham kept his final destination in view as he exercised his faith:

*By faith Abraham, when called to go to a place he would later receive as his inheritance, obeyed and went, even though he did not know where he was going. By faith he made his home in the promise land like a stranger in a foreign country; he lived in tents, as did Isaac and Jacob, who were heirs with him of the same promise. **For he was looking forward to the city with foundations, whose architect and builder is God*** (Hebrews 11:8-10).

God may not ask you to leave your country, your people, or your family, but God is asking you to follow Him—*wherever* He leads. And just as Abraham followed God through a wilderness to his Promised Land, you can take hold of the same kind of faith. Our journey is headed toward our Promised Land—though the route may first take us through valleys, into some battles with giants, and cause us to leave some things behind.

God *did* fulfill His promise to Abraham and made him the physical father of the Jewish nation and also the spiritual father to all believers. However, this did not come easily. As the story continues, we discover the *amazing* depth of Abraham's faith in God.

✟ *Some time later God tested Abraham. He said to him "Abraham!"*
"Here I am," he replied. Then God said "Take your son, your only son,
Isaac, whom you love, and go to the region of Moriah. Sacrifice him
there as a burnt offering on one of the mountains I will tell you about"
(Genesis 22:1-2).

Did you feel the weight of that request as you read it? God asked
Abraham to give up his only son—something God Himself would do for
all of us. How did Abraham feel about God's request? He loved Isaac and
believed the promised "great nation" would be fulfilled through Isaac, his
son. Did Abraham wonder if God was asking him to give up his destiny?

Abraham faced a choice between God's will and his own will. You will
face that choice often on a smaller scale, and maybe someday at this same
magnitude. God may ask you to destroy your view of the future so He can
build a better one—the one you were designed and destined for. He loves
you and you are His creation, therefore, He knows the perfect future for
you. God's plan for your future is often beyond your comprehension.
Sometimes you need to "bite the bullet" and trust God. You will have to
combine *"action"* with your faith to bring it alive.

✟ *You foolish man, do you want evidence that faith without deeds is*
useless? Was not our ancestor Abraham considered righteous for what
he did when he offered his son Isaac on the altar? You see that his
faith and his actions were working together, and his faith was made
complete by what he did. And the scripture was fulfilled that says,
"Abraham believed God, and it was credited to him as righteousness,"
and he was called God's friend. You see that a person is justified by
what he does and not by faith alone...As the body without the spirit
is dead, so faith without deeds is dead (James 2:20-24,26).

Let's continue with Abraham's story.

✞ *When they reached the place God had told him about, Abraham built an altar there and arranged the wood on it. He bound his son Isaac and laid him on the altar, on top of the wood. Then he reached out his hand and took the knife to slay his son. But the angel of the Lord called out to him from Heaven, "Abraham! Abraham!" "Here I am," he replied. "Do not lay a hand on the boy," he said. "Do not do anything to him. Now I know that you fear God, because you have not withheld from Me your son, your only son." Abraham looked up and there in a thicket he saw a ram caught by its horns. He went over and took the ram and sacrificed it as a burnt offering instead of his son. So Abraham called that place The Lord Will Provide. And to this day it is said, "On the mountain of the Lord it will be provided"* (Genesis 22:9-14).

This is a powerful passage and a prophetic snapshot of the ultimate sacrifice God made when He gave His only son Jesus to redeem the world. Abraham was willing to sacrifice his only son, yet God provided an alternate sacrifice—a lamb, symbolic of Jesus—so Abraham's lineage could live on eternally. Note Abraham's words to us: "God will provide." God's provision is the subject of chapters in Book Two. For now, just know that even in the toughest and most challenging circumstances, God will provide a way. God expects you to trust the story of Abraham and others in the Bible to build your confidence.

✞ *These things happen to them* [faith heroes in the Bible] *as examples and were written down as warnings for us, on whom the fulfillment of the ages has come. So, if you think you are standing firm, be careful that you don't fall! No temptation has seized you except what is common to man. And God is faithful; He will not let you be tempted beyond what you can bear. But when you are tempted, He will also provide a way out so that you can stand up under it* (1 Corinthians 10:11-13).

TURNING DEFEAT INTO VICTORY

It was the morning of Jesus' crucifixion and Pilate spoke to the people:

✝ *"But you have a custom that I should release someone to you at the Passover. Do you therefore want me to release to you the King of the Jews [Jesus]?" Then they all cried again, saying, "Not this Man, but Barabbas!" Now Barabbas was a robber* (John 18:39-40 NKJV).

Not only was Barabbas a robber, but in Luke 23:25 he is also described as a lawless man and murderer. You could say Barabbas represented satan (who is described in John 10:10 as a thief, in Matthew 16:23 as a lawless man, and in John 8:44 as a murderer). That morning the choice Pilate was giving humankind was between the only begotten Son of God, whom they had seen bring healing and love into the world, or the crowd could choose satan who brought theft, murder, and lawlessness. As in the Garden, Adam and Eve made the wrong choice. They too chose what satan offered them over what God offered. Humanity sent God's only Son—the only sinless Man, guilty of nothing—to His death on the Cross.

It would have seemed to Jesus' followers that Jesus' death would be the ultimate defeat of His movement and ministry—but the story doesn't end here. There was a bigger spiritual reality taking place that the world did not see. It's not the end of your story either, because there is always a greater spiritual reality taking place. Jesus took the punishment for your sin that day, bringing you back into right-standing with God. Then, three days later, He defeated sin and death to rise from the dead. This is why your story isn't over—Jesus' sacrifice and resurrection gives you eternal life and His resurrection power within you as well as the opportunity to eventually be transformed into the image and likeness of God.

What looked like the greatest defeat ever became God's greatest victory—salvation for you and me. God uses the actions of His adversaries to defeat them and He will use the actions of your adversaries to allow you to defeat them, too.

You may have been surprised to see among the gifts adversity as one of the 12 Gifts of Freedom I believe God offers. Just consider this, Jesus had 12 disciples to help Him change an entire world forever. One of those 12 betrayed Jesus, causing Him the biggest adversity in His life—Jesus' physical death. However, wrapped in that very adversity was Jesus' greatest *victory*—defeat of sin and death in the world—*our redemption*. You have been offered 12 gifts to bring God to your world, and one is wrapped in adversity.

Because of the resurrection power within *you*—your seemingly greatest adversities can become your biggest victories. Look at Abraham and Jesus—when you're willing to give up your future, God can give you the destiny He designed especially for you. Even death is a victory for those who follow Christ—a big step closer to our Promised Land in Heaven and eternal life with God!

Sometimes we practice an uncertain or tentative faith—we believe God's Spirit can breathe resurrection power into one or two specific areas of our lives, yet we feel other areas are hopelessly dead, or we can handle things better than God. However, Jesus wants us to harness His resurrection power in our lives *completely*. The same Spirit who raised Him from the dead is in us. With this power, we can bring to life all that seems dead.

ACTION & VISUALIZATION

In your worst times, look for your victory.

RESURRECTION POWER

There is a story in the Bible about a friend of Jesus' named Lazarus. Lazarus had two sisters, Mary and Martha. Lazarus became sick and ultimately died. But when he first became sick, the two sisters sent a messenger to Jesus.

✞ *So the sisters sent word to Jesus, "Lord, the one you love is sick." When He heard this, Jesus said, "This sickness will not end in death. No, it is for God's glory so that God's Son may be glorified through it"* (John 11:3-4).

Again we see God's plan to use someone's sickness for a greater glory. You may ask, "Who brings sickness and death—God?" I say no. Satan and man bring sickness and death.

✞ *...He [satan] was a murderer from the beginning, not holding to the truth, for there is no truth in Him...* (John 8:44).

✞ *For the wages of sin is death...* (Romans 6:23).

Our sin brought on sickness and death, and indeed God sacrificed His only Son to reverse this curse we have brought on ourselves.

✞ *The thief comes only to steal, kill and destroy: I have come that they may have **life** and have it to the **full*** (John 10:10).

Though God may implant redemption in them, He is not the root cause of sickness and death in our lives.

Read what happens next in the story of Lazarus:

☩ *Jesus loved Martha and her sister and Lazarus. Yet when he heard that Lazarus was sick, He stayed where He was two more days* (John 11:5-6).

Yes, He loved them, but even though He knew Lazarus was near death, He waited *two days* before going to him. Surely the messenger would have had time to report what Jesus said to Mary and Martha—Lazarus would not die! But why the two-day wait? You would think if Jesus loved him and knew Lazarus was sick, He would have left immediately. Jesus' disciples were probably confused by this delay as well:

☩ *After He had said this, He went on to tell them, "Our friend Lazarus has fallen asleep; but I am going there to wake him up." His disciples replied, "Lord, if he sleeps, he will get better." Jesus had been speaking of his death, but His disciples thought He meant natural sleep. So then He told them plainly, "Lazarus is dead, and for your sake I am **glad** I was not there, so that you may believe. But let us go to him"* (John 11:11-15).

Jesus knew this unfolding story was bigger and more important than Lazarus' sickness or even death. Why was He *glad* that he wasn't there when Lazarus was dying? I think it's so He could *bring His disciples' faith alive* along with *Lazarus*. Jesus would demonstrate for them the resurrection power that would change their lives and *yours* too. The story continues:

☩ *Then Thomas (called Didymus) said to the rest of the disciples, "Let us also go, that we may die with him." On His arrival, Jesus found that Lazarus had already been in the tomb for four days. Bethany was less than two miles from Jerusalem, and many Jews had come to Martha and Mary to comfort them in the loss of their brother* (John 11:16-19).

There is great encouragement in these verses—they remind us that we are not alone in our journey. There are many other believers who are ready to comfort and walk alongside you in difficult times. However, make sure you are not burying something God wishes to be alive, like His promise.

✠ *When Martha heard that Jesus was coming, she went out to meet Him, but Mary stayed at home. "Lord," Martha said to Jesus, "if You had been here, my brother would not have died. But I know that even now God will give You whatever You ask. Jesus said to her, "Your brother will rise again." Martha answered, "I know he will rise again in the resurrection at the last day." Jesus said to her, "I am the resurrection and the life. He who believes in Me, though he may die, he shall live. And whoever lives and believes in Me shall never die. Do you believe this?" "Yes, Lord," she told him, "I believe that You are the Christ, the Son of God, who was to come into the world"* (John 11:20-27).

Here's what I find most interesting about this passage: Martha doesn't really answer Jesus' question. She says what is certainly an important belief—*You are the Christ*—yet seemingly ignores the resurrection truth. Isn't this the way many people approach their faith? They believe that Jesus is the Christ—the Savior—but they don't understand or embrace the resurrection power that He brings into their lives.

The apostle Paul spoke about getting hold of this power.

✠ *I want to know Christ **and** the power of the resurrection **and** the fellowship of sharing in His sufferings, becoming like Him in death, and so somehow, to attain to the resurrection from the dead* (Philippians 3:10-11).

The story goes on to say that Martha told her sister Mary that Jesus had arrived. Mary went to Jesus:

✝ *When Mary reached the place where Jesus was and saw Him, she fell at His feet and said, "Lord, if you had been here, my brother would not have died." When Jesus saw her weeping, and the Jews who had come along with her also weeping, he was deeply moved in spirit and troubled* (John 11:32-33).

Jesus was sad, certainly, but I believe He was most troubled by their lack of faith. He had faith He would raise Lazarus from the dead. So He was not mourning the loss of Lazarus, but was mourning their lack of faith. Didn't they know He was the Son of God? Couldn't the Creator of life bring Lazarus back to life? Jesus became even more troubled when He saw they had buried Lazarus, essentially rolling a stone in front of the promises that God made to them:

✝ *Jesus, once more deeply moved, came to the tomb. It was a cave with a stone laid across the entrance. "Take away the stone," he said. "But, Lord," said Martha, the sister of the dead man, "by this time there is a bad odor, for he has been there four days"* (John 11:38-39).

Some of the promises God made to you have been locked away so long that they are dead and stink; however, this does not mean they can't be brought to life by the resurrection power of Jesus. Remember the message Jesus sent?

✝ *Then Jesus said, "Did I not tell you that if you believed, you would see the glory of God?"* (John 11:40)

In the face of adversity if you believe in His power and that His power is in you, then you too can see the glory of God manifest in your life.

✠ *So they took away the stone. Then Jesus looked up and said, "Father, I thank You that You have heard Me. I knew that You always hear Me, but I said this for the benefit of the people standing here, that they may believe that You sent Me." When He had said this, Jesus called in a loud voice, "Lazarus, come out!" The dead man came out, his hands and feet wrapped with strips of linen, and a cloth around his face. Jesus said to them, "Take off the grave clothes and let him go"* (John 11:41-44).

When you act on your faith, you can be in a place to receive God's promises in your life.

✠ *...The Lord is faithful to all His promises and loving toward all He has made* (Psalm 145:13).

ACTION & VISUALIZATION

Jesus said, "I am the resurrection and the life.
He who believes in Me will live even though He dies;
and whoever lives and believes in Me will never die."
Do you believe this?

Do you believe Jesus is working in the midst of your adversity? Do you believe the valley you may be walking through right now is not your home? Do you believe God can resurrect that seemingly lifeless circumstance in your life?

It is only to the degree that you have faith in God's love for you that you can clearly see the gift He implants into adversities. Reacting to these adversities with actions of faith allows you to receive the gifts of God within.

Words such as *faith* and *belief* may be easy to read off the page and nice to think about, but they may be hard to practice and live out. But remember, we are called to a *living faith* and in the midst of adversity our living faith can truly come to life where there was once death—radiating God's presence for the world to see.

MEDITATION POINT

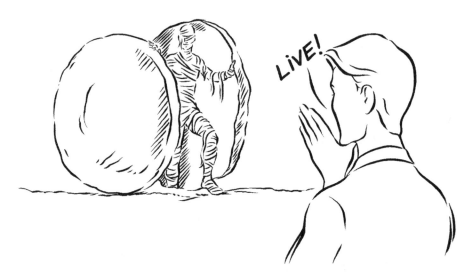

Your faith in action will manifest God's promises to come alive in your life.

Go to Chapter 8 in the Study Guide section on page 311.

ENDNOTE

1. Jack Hayford, ed., *Spirit Filled Life Bible for Students* (Nashville, TN: Thomas Nelson Publishers, 1995), 1443.

Study Guide

INTRODUCTION

Please don't think of this study guide as a homework assignment. It *isn't* about giving the "right answer"—it's about giving an honest answer. It *isn't* about "getting it done"—it's about letting the questions stir your heart. It *isn't* about "filling in the blanks"—but instead letting the Holy Spirit speak to your soul. Think of this as a spiritual experience or potential encounter between you and God rather than an exercise to check off your "to do" list.

We are conditioned to believe that our answers to questions in a textbook will be graded; however, that mindset stifles the purpose of this study guide. This is an opportunity to write honestly about your faith, to grow and go deeper in God's Word, to pray earnestly about His will for your life, and most of all to cultivate an intimate relationship between you and your Creator.

If possible, devote time for quiet reflection as you read the material, think about your life, and write accordingly. Answer the questions as you truly feel, even if it seems wrong or troubling. Remember that "the truth will set you free" and growth can only happen when the soil is soft. You get what you give. You could burn through this entire study guide in half an hour if you like, but it would offer little to no lasting benefit.

I pray that you will put in the time and effort to maximize this material and actualize the full impact of His Gifts of Freedom into your life.

Use the Study Guide to find the spiritual growth and maturity God desires you to have in your life.

The Gifts of Freedom Study Guide

BOOK ONE

GIFTS OF LIFE, HOLY SPIRIT, FAITH, AND ADVERSITY

HOW TO USE THE STUDY GUIDE

You can use this study guide in a variety of ways, including individually, as part of a small group Bible study, or in a Sunday school setting. If you are working through this book on your own, use this study guide to record your personal growth journey. Take the time after each chapter to answer the questions. Some are designed to help you remember the main concepts in the chapter, while others are designed to help you personalize the content and apply it to your own life. At the end seriously pray in closing that God will fill you with His gifts—and that you will recognize and accept them. You can also visit our Website (www.giftsoffreedom.com) and see how others have applied this information to their lives.

If you're reading this book in a small group, use the study questions to prompt lively discussion. Discuss the action steps with at least one other group member to build accountability in your plans for action, then close your time together with prayer. For more information on how to lead a group or Sunday school class and get additional resources, visit our Website at www.giftsoffreedom.com.

If you are not currently in a group study of the book, you might want to consider starting one after you finish, so you can spread to others the new freedoms you have discovered. As you help others, you will deepen your understanding and relationship with God—gaining even more freedoms.

Go to www.giftsoffreedom.com for additional resource materials and instructions.

Chapter 1

IN THE BEGINNING...
WHAT'S MY PURPOSE AND WHAT WENT WRONG?

STUDY QUESTIONS

1. What was God's original plan when He created man?

   _____

   _____

   _____

   _____

2. What changed, and how does that change (the Fall) affect your life on a daily basis?

   _____

   _____

   _____

   _____

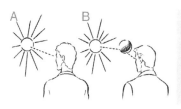

Light allows you to see the physical world if you open your eyes, and God allows you to see the spiritual realm if you open your spiritual eyes. His light is required for your insight.

3. It takes light for you to physically see. Do you need His light for better spiritual insight? Why is His light so important for us to see spiritual things?

_____

_____

_____

The universe is based on "cause and effect"—all your actions come back to you.

4. What does the Law of Cause and Effect say? Who is responsible for your life? For your spiritual growth?

_____

_____

_____

_____

_____

God's beautiful illustration of the kind of metamorphosis, we too can choose to experience – a spiritual then physical metamorphosis.

5. How is the butterfly's metamorphosis similar to the way Christians grow into the people God created them to be?

_____

_____

_____

A   B

You must plug in to shine His light.

6. Why did God make us in His image and likeness? Where do you see His image and likeness manifesting itself in your own life? Any areas it is not?

_____

_____

_____

_____

_____

Playing the role of the victim will lead you down the wrong path in life.

7. Why did Adam and Eve's sin (the Fall) ruin their relationship with their Creator? Have you ever felt distant from God? Was it your actions or God's that prompted that feeling?

_____

_____

_____

8. What was satan's strategy to lure Adam and Eve into sin? Does satan use this strategy in your life? If so, how does he tempt or lure you away from God?

_____

_____

_____

9. Can a person really hide from God? What are some of the ways you try to hide from God?

_____

_____

_____

_____

10. Respond to the following quote: "God's priority is our spiritual side, not the physical fulfillment and obsession with our bodies' needs..." How might this play out in your life?

_____

_____

_____

_____

_____

_____

11. What is the difference between God creating us with free will versus God creating us like "sock puppets"? Why wouldn't God just program us to love Him?

_____

_____

_____

_____

_____

_____

His blood covers your sin so that when God looks at you He only sees Jesus' righteousness.

12. To have a perfect world, wouldn't we all need to act according to His image and likeness? Do you see the need for the consequences of sin to be death so the cancer of evil won't last forever? Is a just God required for us to live in a just world? In what ways and why? How did God satisfy justice and love at the same time?

_____

_____

ACTION STEPS

Summarize the content of Chapter 1. Based on what you've learned, do you know God better? Do you understand His path, essence, intent, and His plan for you? What are things you can do in the pursuit of His destiny for you?

_____

_____

CLOSING PRAYER

(Pray this prayer or pray your own to close this study time.)

Lord, thank You for the Gifts of Freedom. Open my heart and mind as I begin to learn more about these gifts and how they can help me reconnect with Your Spirit.

Chapter 2

GIFT #1—LIFE (PART 1)
HOW DO YOU GET IT?

STUDY QUESTIONS

1. What memories do you have of unwrapping gifts when you were a child? Why does God desire a childlike nature from His children?

_____

_____

_____

_____

2. The first Gift of Freedom is life—salvation. How much work do I need to do before I can receive this gift? Why should I open it first?

_____

_____

_____

_____

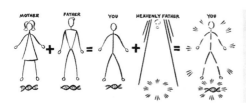

Your parents can only give you what they have as fallible (fallen) human beings. However what God adds makes the new eternal you.

3. Why would the first gift be called Life if we already have it? How is the kind of life God offers different from your current existence?

_____

_____

_____

Clean drinking water is polluted by poison we dump into the stream.

4. What does the image in this diagram say about sin? Can God drink of an intimate relationship with us in our present condition? What is the only way to purify our reservoir?

_____

_____

_____

_____

You must not just believe Jesus existed and is great but also that He is the only one who will get you across to your salvation.

5. What is grace? Why is grace important in salvation? Can we save ourselves? Why not?

_____

_____

_____

A   B   C

Pull yourself closer to the source (God) and your light will shine brighter.

6. What role does our salvation play in beginning our relationship with God? In exuding His image in likeness? How do we continue to work out our salvation?

_____

_____

_____

_____

7. Is it possible to accept the gift of life on fact or evidence alone, or do we need faith? Once accepted, will God give us assurances when we ask?

_____

_____

_____

An accidental or purposeful creation?

8. When looking at God's creation, why is it hard to believe that there is no Creator? What evidence do you find in creation that God exists and loves you?

_____

_____

_____

9. What is one way that you personally have seen God speaking and revealing Himself in His creation?

_____

_____

_____

Flying blind is dangerous for you and others – aboard your plane.

10. How does your physical mind and body distract you from the spiritual? What part does your spirit play in helping you navigate through life? How do you find the eternal?

_____

_____

_____

_____

_____

11. Is it difficult for you to believe that God accepts you the way you are? Why or why not?

_____

_____

_____

_____

_____

Satan does not want you to shine God's light into the world.

12. Do you think satan is attacking God's seeds growing in you? Is there anything you can do about it? What is your counter-attack plan?

_____

_____

_____

ACTION STEPS

Have you received and opened the first gift? If not, what is stopping you from accepting and unwrapping the gift of salvation? If you have, what does this change mean in your daily life? What changes do you see coming as you seek to grow spiritually? Make a plan for how you will begin to grow and write your initial thoughts here.

_____

_____

CLOSING PRAYER

(Pray this prayer or pray your own to close this study time.)

Lord, thank You for the gift of life. Help me to accept it by faith and learn to avoid the temptations satan puts in my way as I seek to grow closer to You.

Chapter 3

Gift #1—Life (Part 2)

How do you get the most from it?

Study Questions

1. In what ways can you relate to the "now what" question at the beginning of this chapter? Is it clear to you now how you will get the answer to that question? What are some of the ways He will use to provide the answers?

_____

_____

_____

_____

_____

_____

_____

_____

_____

_____

You will never get a firm hold on worldly happiness, so stop running in vain and look inside to find joy.

2. What are three things you are pursuing in your life? Ultimately, what do you plan to gain from these pursuits? How have you made the pursuit of happiness a priority in your life? What do you think should be your highest priority? What can you do to start pursuing this priority?

_____

_____

_____

_____

_____

3. Using the analogy of preparing for a race, what are you doing today to prepare for eternal life? What things are you starting? What things are you stopping to make room for those things you are starting?

_____

_____

_____

_____

_____

 Don't isolate yourself, stay where it is hot!

4. How does finding and attending a church help you "stay hot" in your faith? Is it possible to "stay hot" and be alone, isolated from other believers? Why or why not? What are other important aspects of finding a good church?

_____

_____

5. What does baptism symbolize? What are some other actions we can take that symbolize and memorialize our life-changing decisions?

_____

_____

6. Why do you think the Bible uses the phrase "new creation" when describing a follower of Jesus? What has God changed or made new in you? What aspect of your life has not changed immediately and is left up to you?

_____

_____

7. What are some of the ways we can take advantage of our new life?

_____

_____

Prepare yourself to start running beneficial mental programs. Your actions will follow.

8. Consider the fact that the Bible is an ancient Book. So, why is it still relevant to us today? What makes the Bible so special? How does God use it to affect the way we live today?

_____

_____

_____

Even time itself revolves around Jesus.

9. What kind of relationship does Jesus want you to have with Him? What are some of your personal obstacles that can get in the way?

_____

_____

_____

_____

_____

He wants to focus with you on where you are going.

10. How does your past factor into this relationship?

_____

_____

_____

 =

His image and likeness in you is essentially your relationship with Him.

11. List some things that come to mind when you think of Jesus. Is this accurate with the Biblical account of His life and ministry? Write four reasons why you believe it is important to walk in the image and likeness of Jesus.

_____

_____

_____

_____

_____

12. Respond to this statement: "God is most interested in who you are—not what you do." What does God think of "who you are"? Can you find Scripture support for your answer?

_____

_____

_____

Action Steps

Think about what it means to embrace the "new life" you've been given. What are some practical things you can do to become more like Jesus? Are there some habits you need to change? How might you begin reprogramming yourself to change those habits? List those action steps here.

_____

_____

_____

Closing Prayer

(Pray this prayer or pray your own to close this study time.)

Lord, You have made me a new creation. Help me to take steps toward living out that new creation in daily life. Give me wisdom as I seek to become more like You everyday.

Chapter 4

GIFT #2—THE HOLY SPRIT (PART 1)
WHAT DOES THE HOLY SPIRIT MEAN IN YOUR LIFE?

STUDY QUESTIONS

1. Why does Jesus offer us the Holy Spirit? How is this a "new connection with God"? What is the Holy Spirit's role in your life?

_____

_____

_____

_____

_____

_____

_____

_____

_____

The Holy Spirit lets you see God's perspective above your grounded state.

2. Which word used to describe the Holy Spirit has the most meaning to you right now? (Some examples: Comforter, Helper, Advocate, Guide, etc.) Why did you choose this word?

_____

_____

_____

Follow the Holy Spirit's signs, they lead to becoming in His image and likeness. Any other way will eventually lead to death.

3. What are some areas of your life that could use divine help, guidance, or council? Do you know some ways the Holy Spirit will speak to you? List them.

_____

_____

_____

_____

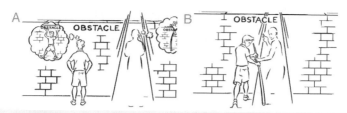

Only God can show you the way through your obstacles in life—turn dead ends into beginnings—death to life.

4. Given the fact that God knows everything and is all-powerful, can you see areas in your life where He could provide supernatural resurrection power?

_____

_____

5. Read again the Scripture passages in The Power of the Spirit section of this chapter. Which verses speak to you most powerfully about your life? Why? Have you fully considered how other passages may apply to your life?

_____

_____

_____

6. Is it possible for you to receive and understand spiritual things without the help of the Holy Spirit? How can we be open to the Holy Spirit's revelation even when it may seem hard to believe considering our experiences or circumstances?

_____

_____

_____

7. Have you ever felt prompted by the Holy Spirit? Describe that experience. If not, in what areas of your life do you hope to experience His prompting?

_____

_____

_____

God will expose you to what you will need to know when you're capable of using it. You will need to pay attention at all times and be open to learning or you will not have the information when you need it.

8. How can it be difficult or even troubling to wait on "God's timing"? Why is God's timing perfect and how does faith play a role in waiting?

_____

_____

_____

9. Consider the story of the man in the flood. What kind of crisis do you face today? What are three ways God could provide a way out or might already be answering the request? Could something you need to do be the answer? Are you looking and open to perceive Him in your circumstances?

_____

_____

_____

God places information for you everywhere, if you're looking and open to it.

10. Does God bring us divine insight and information in places beyond church? Is it difficult to separate God information from worldly information? Why?

_____

_____

_____

When you seek answers as to your direction, God will provide them if you look for them.

11. What are some of the sins in your life where you may have developed a callous to the Holy Spirit's leading? How can and will you change toward becoming open again to Him speaking to you in these areas?

_____

_____

_____

_____

12. At the end of the chapter, the verse in Matthew says "narrow is the road that leads to life and few find it." Why do you think only "a few" find the road to life? Are you striving to be one of the few as quoted in this passage?

_____

_____

_____

Action Steps

Think about what you've learned about the Holy Spirit's role in your life. What are some things you know now that can help you grow closer to God? List some practical things you can do to better understand the Holy Spirit's role, and to pursue the wisdom, comfort, and guidance He offers.

_____

_____

_____

Closing Prayer

(Pray this prayer or pray your own to close this study time.)

Father, thank You for the gift of the Holy Spirit. Lead me in my understanding of the Spirit's role in my life and help me to see and hear His promptings.

Chapter 5

Gift #2—The Holy Sprit (Part 2)
How do you make the Holy Spirit relevant in your life?

STUDY QUESTIONS

1. In the Great Commission, Jesus says, "Go and make disciples." Does this mean we are single-handedly responsible to convince and force people to become disciples? What is a disciple? How are true disciples made? In what ways can you be part of that process?

_____

_____

_____

_____

_____

_____

_____

People can argue about your doctrine and religion but they can't argue with your experience because you're the sole expert. They didn't experience it.

2. If you've accepted Christ, you already have a story. In as few words as possible, tell that story here.

_____

_____

_____

_____

_____

_____

3. List some of the people in your life who have not heard your story/testimony. How do you think they would respond? Have you worked out a plan with the Holy Spirit to share your story with each of them?

_____

_____

_____

_____

_____

_____

Do the part you are assigned and let God orchestrate the rest.

4. If we plant "spiritual seed" and see little or no growth, what does that mean? What can we do to till the ground? How can timing be a factor? Once a seed starts taking root how can we water it?

_____

_____

_____

5. Is boldness really God-given? If so, when does God give you supernatural boldness? What would that look like in real life for you?

_____

_____

_____

6. Does the Holy Spirit offer His power only to overseas missionaries, pastors, and heroes in the Bible? Why will the Holy Spirit offer this same power to you?

_____

_____

_____

_____

Imagine for a minute the world God desired you to live in where everyone treated you with real love. Do your part now to start bringing that world into existence—it's called heaven on earth.

7. What is Jesus talking about when He instructs us to "Bear much fruit"? How do we do this, and why is it important?

_____

_____

_____

A

B

Stay on the path called "His will" where the obstacles have already been worked out for you.

8. What does it mean to "subject your will" to God? When you do so does that mean you want to encounter obstacles in life? Why will the Holy Spirit offer His power and assistance when you're operating in "God's will"?

_____

_____

_____

9. Which is more valuable in your life: "wisdom" or "knowledge"? What are the qualities and characteristics that separate the two? Have you witnessed wisdom instead of knowledge emerging in your own life? How will it help you in decisions to ask yourself this question, "What would be the wise thing to do?"

_____

_____

Follow the Holy Spirit into battles to possess your promised land.

10. What is the third step in the progression of faith? How does this memorialize your relationship? You are already a Christian and have the Holy Spirit dwelling in you, so why should you be baptized in the Spirit?

_____

_____

Let God speak directly from His Spirit ot your's without interference.

11. What are the benefits of praying in the Spirit if any?

_____

12. In what ways does the Holy Spirit help prepare you to receive the other gifts of the Spirit?

_____

_____

_____

ACTION STEPS

If you haven't yet received the baptism of the Spirit, meet with other Christians to learn what you must do to embrace this baptism. Also, if you haven't been water baptized, consider the steps necessary to doing this at your church.

Review your answer to question 2. Think of ways you can share this story in everyday circumstances. Though it's best to tell your story naturally (not in a scripted manner), it might help to say it out loud a few times so you can think about the things that matter most, and organize it in a way that is simple to understand. Consider "role-playing" a conversation where you have an opportunity to share your testimony with another believer.

_____

_____

CLOSING PRAYER

(Pray this prayer or pray your own to close this study time.)

Father, thank You for the many ways the Holy Spirit partners with me as I seek to gain the freedom You desire for me. Help me to receive and embrace the Holy Spirit as I continue to grow my intimate relationship with You.

Chapter 6

GIFT #3—FAITH (PART 1)
WHY IS FAITH NEEDED TO UNITE GOD'S GIFTS?

STUDY QUESTIONS

It takes faith to please God so when we are living our lives by faith we are pleasing God all the time.

1. Is faith something you can acquire or receive through personal prayer, teaching, and study? If not, where does it come from and how do you make it work for you?

_____

_____

2. The Bible says, "without faith it is impossible to please God." Can't you simply please God by "being good" and going to church? How do you personally live by faith? What does that look like in your life?

_____

_____

"No pain, no gain"; however when you do gain you please God.

3. If exercising your faith is similar to physical exercise, what causes you to "break a sweat" spiritually speaking? What benefits do you receive from this exercise and how do you receive them?

_____

_____

_____

Praying in what you hope for is an action of faith.

4. How does the analogy of the Grand Canyon apply to faith? What does it mean in your life to "pack the car" or "fill it with gas" etc.? Briefly describe a few ways you have acted or will act in faith?

_____

_____

_____

_____

5. Most people take great care and pride in their homes. Most would never invest money in a property with a bad, unstable foundation. Yet, what are some ways that you have invested in property built on sand?

_____

_____

_____

Have faith in going down God's path for that is where your Heavenly Father has hidden your rewards.

6. Do you have faith to stay on the path God lays out for you until you reach your reward? What about when the path is tiring or painful, or the rewards don't initially seem apparent? How about when you have to wait a long time? Can you think of some examples where you've struggled to walk down God's path of faith?

_____

_____

_____

_____

_____

7. Is it possible for you to find joy in the midst of a trial? Is it possible to "count it pure joy" in the midst of pain? Based on your response to trials, do you think that would change the way others thought of you in those trials? Who is the best source to get answers from when trials come your way?

_____

_____

_____

Look for the opportunity in your trouble—a good attitude alone will always be a witness of Him in you to others.

8. Can having faith in God's good intentions allow you to have joy during troubles? How can faith encourage you to find the good in those trials, or build you up? Can faith encourage you to better please God?

_____

_____

_____

9. How can looking to God's history within the Bible help build your faith?

_____

_____

_____

Are all your beliefs consistent with God's story you're telling.

10. Are you prepared to give an account for the hope you have within you that is consistent with the Bible?

_____

_____

_____

_____

_____

11. The Bible says "Faith without action is dead." You read many stories in the Bible where regular people's actions of faith moved God. What does an action of faith look like in your own life? Think also beyond church-related activities.

_____

_____

_____

_____

_____

_____

What seems bad to you at times often brings good things.

12. Has this fallen world tested your faith through a major trial? Has this change brought you closer to God or have you let it drive you further away? In what ways? How could you have used these circumstances to make your relationship closer and more intimate? Can you visualize this in future circumstances?

_____

_____

ACTION STEPS

What are some ways you currently act on faith? What are practical things you can do to be more intentional in your actions of faith? Are there some things you're currently struggling with that you need to trust God for? List those things here and take a moment to pray for faith and God's will in these areas of your life.

_____

_____

CLOSING PRAYER

(Pray this prayer or pray your own to close this study time.)

Father, thank You for the gift of faith. Help me to grow in faith and learn to trust You with the things I don't understand.

Chapter 7

GIFT #3—FAITH (PART 2)
HOW CAN YOU STRENGTHEN YOUR FAITH?

STUDY QUESTIONS

1. In Matthew 17:20, Jesus says with faith "nothing is impossible for you." If you believed this without reservation, what would change?

_____

_____

_____

_____

2. What does it take to get mountain-moving faith? Is mountain-moving faith different from what you are doing now? Why? What are the key components to a mountain-moving faith?

_____

_____

_____

_____

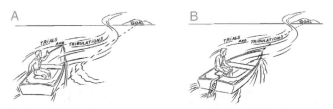

Your unwavering faith will act as a rudder to keep you on course.

3. How can pockets of doubt affect your mind, desires, heart, words, and actions? How can that affect your faith?

_____

_____

_____

_____

_____

4. What does it mean to "align your words and heart"? How do you do that? Write an example of this from your life.

_____

_____

_____

_____

_____

Faithless words can stop you from reaching your goals.

5. Our faithless speech has an impact on our heart and mind. Are there some nonverbal ways you live faithlessly? What can you do to change?

_____

_____

_____

A   B

To reach your goals you need a clear vision of who you are in Christ. This will then be reflected in your actions and the results you achieve.

6. How can you use the visualization process to get to the place God wants you to be? How will you work this into your daily life?

_____

_____

7. Respond to this statement: A real relationship with God demands that you line up your actions each day, not just when it seems convenient.

_____

_____

He is there all the time wanting to be engaged in your life.

8. What are ways you can develop a daily, ongoing connection with God's presence? If this is something you would like, what are some steps you can take?

_____

_____

_____

_____

_____

9. Do you see examples in your life of the "five challenges" to your faith discussed in the chapter? List examples in your life of each of the challenges.

_____

_____

_____

_____

_____

"When you hit bumps in life, does God's love come out of you"?

10. Do you hear what God is saying to you through your daily circumstances? Are you making a genuine attempt to listen? List some areas where you think God may be speaking to you (i.e., job, friendship, family, events, etc).

_____

_____

_____

There is resurrection power in your testimony.

11. What was your reaction to the story of the lame man at the gate called Beautiful? Maybe you're not paralyzed, but in what way could your life be related to his?

_____

_____

_____

_____

12. Does God ultimately offer us grace and mercy with the thoughts, actions, and habits we're having trouble eliminating? Why? What is ultimately most important to Him?

_____

_____

_____

_____

ACTION STEPS

List some of the current struggles you're facing in life. Could they be pointing you back to God? Think of the caterpillar and its struggle from cocoon to flight. How does your faith in God's good intentions help you deal with those struggles? Are there things you can do today to help build a stronger faith for facing difficult times? Make a note of those here.

_____

_____

_____

_____

CLOSING PRAYER

(Pray this prayer or pray your own to close this study time.)

Lord, thank You for placing a gift in all the struggles I'm facing, and for letting me know how I can unwrap them. Help me align my heart and actions so they are in line with Your will for my life.

Chapter 8

GIFT #4—ADVERSITY

HOW CAN FAITH TURN ADVERSITY INTO VICTORY?

STUDY QUESTIONS

1. Does God bring adversity, or do you mostly bring it on yourself? When you do something stupid that causes adversity, does God put some form of gift in it to offer you redemption?

_____

_____

_____

_____

2. If you are facing adversity, has God turned His back on you? If God is good and loving, why does He allow adversity into your life?

_____

_____

_____

_____

Everybody knows experience helps you reach your goals in life and that will help you reach your purpose.

3. What are some of the gifts God puts within adversities that can help strengthen and redeem your life and relationship with Him?

_____

_____

4. List the adversities you are facing right now. Will you look for a gift in them?

_____

_____

5. Are you letting life experiences govern your attitude and vision? In what ways are you letting life circumstances affect you from the outside in? What does a life that works from the inside out look like?

_____

_____

6. Look at the story of David and Goliath. David's character exhibited an extraordinary faith. What are some Goliath-like problems or struggles in your life that seem insurmountable? How could they be strengthening you or creating a testimony?

_____

_____

7. How did David develop his faith over time? How did overcoming the problems build up his faith? What made him different from the others in Saul's army? What makes you different from the rest of the world?

_____

_____

_____

Act in faith when you're hit. Act in faith when you get knocked down. Act in faith when God provides the path to victory even if it seems unusual.

8. In your trials, battles, and adversities, are you open to using untraditional weapons or solutions that God may offer you? Like David, are you open to creating a new testimony with Him?

_____

_____

_____

_____

_____

  Abraham was willing and Jesus was willing in faith to sacrifice their futures for God's will in their lives, are you?

9. What causes you to doubt? What is the remedy for that doubt?

_____

_____

_____

_____

_____

_____

10. Consider your own relationship with those you love. How has your faith in them cultivated your relationship? How does this relate to developing intimacy with God?

_____

_____

_____

_____

Your greatest defeat will be your greatest victory!

11. In the case of relationships between a loving Creator and His created, wouldn't it make sense for the created to yield to the Creator for its own good and the good of the relationship? How can you align yourself with God's will today? What areas in your life are you currently holding off limits?

_____

_____

_____

_____

_____

12. God's resurrection power turns adversity into victory. How do you turn adversity into victory? What are some areas of your life that need victory?

_____

_____

_____

_____

_____

ACTION STEPS

Spend some time reading about David's faith. Consider what impresses you most about his actions. What can you learn from his faith? How can you work toward building up a similar faith? If there are some obstacles or adversities in your life today, think of ways to use them for your benefit. List your thoughts here.

_____

_____

_____

_____

_____

_____

_____

_____

_____

CLOSING PRAYER

(Pray this prayer or pray your own to close this study time.)

Father, thank You so much for the gift of faith and the role it plays in helping me open the gift of adversity. Allow me to clearly see the gifts in all my adversities. Grant me a portion of faith that will allow me to do all those things You desire for me to do, and let me see how to use that faith to accomplish them.

ABOUT THE AUTHOR

Greg Rice began his real estate business in 1971; however, God has taken him on a most unusual journey since then. In 1988, he gave his heart to Jesus Christ—the gift of salvation began to grow, heal, and restore his life. Greg's continual seeking to know God and develop a most intimate relationship with Him has led to many discoveries.

As God was healing him, Greg began to share his new life and success with others through several ministries. Greg has now focused much of his ministry efforts through Solid Rock Media (see www.solidrockmedia.com), and its vision is to illuminate the life and light of Jesus to a dying world through various media outlets.

The Gifts of Freedom book series grew out of this pursuit and in November 2005, the Holy Spirit began to give the words. God's message was clear: "offer Christians a clear path toward living in wholehearted freedom."

God has an answer for those who find themselves bound in life by things not of God. God's desire is for everyone bound and held captive in life to be set free so they can achieve their purpose and fulfill their destiny. The Gifts of Freedom was written for you to know about the gifts God offers so that you can achieve the purpose and calling He has planned for you.

Men and women held in prison also have a God-given purpose and destiny. With this in mind, Greg's mission is to distribute the Gifts of

Freedom free of charge to prisons and jails around the world to facilitate salvation, discipleship, healing, and growth. To this end Greg has already donated 120,000 copies to prisons across the United States.

If you have the resources and God is stirring your heart, please help Greg reach these men and women who are in need of a life-freeing Savior. It is Greg's prayer that the Spirit of God would bring change within, working from the inside out—as only He can bring true rehabilitation and freedom. Partner with Greg by giving a donation to distribute additional copies of the books—bringing spiritual nourishment to spiritually hungry men and women in prisons worldwide. In the U.S. alone there are over 7,000 incarceration facilities now holding almost 3,000,000 prisoners.

Write a check to "Gifts of Freedom" and mail to:

GIFTS OF FREEDOM
PO BOX 62459
COLORADO SPRINGS, CO 80962
VISIT WWW.GIFTSOFFREEDOM.ORG

✠ *I, the Lord, have called you in righteousness; I will take hold of your hand. I will keep you and will make you to be a covenant for the people and a light for the Gentiles, to open eyes that are blind, to free captives from prison and to release from the dungeon those who sit in darkness* (Isaiah 42:6-8).

MINISTRY INFORMATION

Today within the prison system, the news media has focused their attention on over-crowding and violence, but mainly on the lack of true rehabilitation for inmates. While these challenges are very real, we serve a God of redemption—believing that Jesus Christ is the only way to true rehabilitation. Impact for Life ministries believes this Truth must be accessible to inmates and their loved ones through strategic life-giving resources.

While we may read about the 3,000,000 "inmates" or "criminals," these people are not merely numbers in the prison system—they have names, faces, goals, hopes, and families. They are loved and called by God just like you and me. And they need your help. I urge you to partner with Impact for Life as we seek to nurture and disciple men, women, and even children with the saving truth of Jesus Christ.

You can start by visiting the Website. Please consider opening your resources to help bring about change from within.

Please contact:

IMPACT FOR LIFE MINISTRIES
3020 N. EL PASO, SUITE 102
COLORADO SPRINGS, CO 80907
WEBSITE: WWW.IMPACTLIFE.ORG

Additional copies of this book and other
book titles from DESTINY IMAGE are
available at your local bookstore.

Call toll-free: 1-800-722-6774.

Send a request for a catalog to:

Destiny Image® Publishers, Inc.
P.O. Box 310
Shippensburg, PA 17257-0310

*"Speaking to the Purposes of God for This
Generation and for the Generations to Come."*

**For a complete list of our titles,
visit us at www.destinyimage.com.**